God at Work

OTHER TITLES BY BRUCE TAYLOR

The Word in the Wind

No Business as Usual

Looking Up at Love

Life Woven into God

Between Advents

Christ's New Address

Love Walks on Wounded Feet

God at Work

More Sermons for the Lectionary, Year A,
Pentecost through Christ the King

BRUCE L. TAYLOR

WIPF & STOCK · Eugene, Oregon

GOD AT WORK
More Sermons for the Lectionary, Year A, Pentecost through Christ the King

Copyright © 2022 Bruce L. Taylor. All rights reserved. Except for brief quotations in critical publications or reviews, no part of this book may be reproduced in any manner without prior written permission from the publisher. Write: Permissions, Wipf and Stock Publishers, 199 W. 8th Ave., Suite 3, Eugene, OR 97401.

Wipf & Stock
An Imprint of Wipf and Stock Publishers
199 W. 8th Ave., Suite 3
Eugene, OR 97401

www.wipfandstock.com

PAPERBACK ISBN: 978-1-6667-5081-2
HARDCOVER ISBN: 978-1-6667-5082-9
EBOOK ISBN: 978-1-6667-5083-6

OCTOBER 10, 2022 8:00 AM

Unless otherwise noted, scripture quotations are from Common Bible: New Revised Standard Version Bible, copyright © 1989 National Council of the Churches of Christ in the United States of America. Used by permission. All rights reserved worldwide. Emphasis added.

Scripture quotations marked (RSV) are from Revised Standard Version of the Bible, copyright © 1946, 1952, and 1971 National Council of the Churches of Christ in the United States of America. Used by permission. All rights reserved. Emphasis added.

In memory of Ed and Martha Lea Mitchell

Contents

Introduction   xiii

THE DAY OF PENTECOST
First Presbyterian Church, Norfolk, Nebraska, June 3, 1990
Acts 2:1–21; Romans 8:14–17; John 14:8–17, 25–27
"An Experience of Pentecost"   1

TRINITY SUNDAY
First Presbyterian Church, Norfolk, Nebraska, June 10, 1990
Deuteronomy 4:32–40; 2 Corinthians 13:5–14; Matthew 28:16–20
"Experiencing the Faith"   5

EIGHTH SUNDAY IN ORDINARY TIME
Spanish Springs Presbyterian Church, Sparks, Nevada, May 25, 2008
Isaiah 49:8–16a; 1 Corinthians 4:1–5; Matthew 6:24–34
"Consider the Lilies"   11

NINTH SUNDAY IN ORDINARY TIME
Spanish Springs Presbyterian Church, Sparks, Nevada, June 1, 2008
Genesis 6:9–22; 7:24; 8:14–19; Romans 1:16–17; 3:21–31; Matthew 7:21–29
"The Stubborn Creator"   18

TENTH SUNDAY IN ORDINARY TIME
Spanish Springs Presbyterian Church, Sparks, Nevada, June 6, 1999
Genesis 12:1–9; Romans 4:13–25; Matthew 9:9–13, 18–26
"Grace at the Table"   23

ELEVENTH SUNDAY IN ORDINARY TIME
Spanish Springs Presbyterian Church, Sparks, Nevada, June 15, 2008
Genesis 18:1–15; 21:1–7; Romans 5:1–8; Matthew 9:35—10:8
"Absurd Faith"   28

TWELFTH SUNDAY IN ORDINARY TIME
Spanish Springs Presbyterian Church, Sparks, Nevada, June 19, 2005
Genesis 21:8–21; Romans 6:1b–11; Matthew 10:24–39
"Chosenness" — 33

THIRTEENTH SUNDAY IN ORDINARY TIME
First Presbyterian Church, Ponca City, Oklahoma, June 29, 2014
Genesis 22:1–14; Romans 6:12–23; Matthew 10:40–42
"What Sort of a God . . . ?" — 38

FOURTEENTH SUNDAY IN ORDINARY TIME
Spanish Springs Presbyterian Church, Sparks, Nevada, July 3, 2011
Genesis 24:34–38, 42–49, 58–67; Romans 7:15–25a; Matthew 11:16–19, 25–30
"We Are Not Our Savior" — 44

FIFTEENTH SUNDAY IN ORDINARY TIME
Spanish Springs Presbyterian Church, Sparks, Nevada, July 13, 2008
Genesis 25:19–34; Romans 8:1–11; Matthew 13:1–9, 18–23
"The Bible's Brand of Spirituality" — 49

SIXTEENTH SUNDAY IN ORDINARY TIME
First Presbyterian Church, Dodge City, Kansas, July 18, 1993
Genesis 28:10–19a; Romans 8:12–25; Matthew 13:24–30, 36–43
"Parable of a Patient Farmer" — 54

SEVENTEENTH SUNDAY IN ORDINARY TIME
First Presbyterian Church, Dodge City, Kansas, July 28, 1996
Genesis 29:15–28; Romans 8:26–39; Matthew 13:31–33, 44–52
"God at Work" — 59

EIGHTEENTH SUNDAY IN ORDINARY TIME
Spanish Springs Presbyterian Church, Sparks, Nevada, August 1, 1999
Genesis 32:22–31; Romans 9:1–5; Matthew 14:13–21
"Dare to Be Blessed" — 64

NINETEENTH SUNDAY IN ORDINARY TIME
Spanish Springs Presbyterian Church, Sparks, Nevada, August 10, 2008
Genesis 37:1–4, 12–28; Romans 10:5–15; Matthew 14:22–33
"God's Dream" — 70

TWENTIETH SUNDAY IN ORDINARY TIME
First Presbyterian Church, Dodge City, Kansas, August 18, 1996
Genesis 45:1–15; Romans 11:1–2a, 29–32; Matthew 15:10–28
"What *God* Intends" 75

TWENTY-FIRST SUNDAY IN ORDINARY TIME
Spanish Springs Presbyterian Church, Sparks, Nevada, August 21, 2011
Exodus 1:8—2:10; Romans 12:1–8; Matthew 16:13–20
"Testaments to Freedom" 81

TWENTY-SECOND SUNDAY IN ORDINARY TIME
Spanish Springs Presbyterian Church, Sparks, Nevada, August 28, 2011
Exodus 3:1–15; Romans 12:9–21; Matthew 16:21–28
"On Holy Ground" 86

TWENTY-THIRD SUNDAY IN ORDINARY TIME
Spanish Springs Presbyterian Church, Sparks, Nevada, September 8, 2002
Exodus 12:1–14; Romans 13:8–14; Matthew 18:15–20
"Slaves No More" 92

TWENTY-FOURTH SUNDAY IN ORDINARY TIME
Spanish Springs Presbyterian Church, Sparks, Nevada, September 15, 2002
Exodus 14:19–31; Romans 14:1–12; Matthew 18:21–35
"The Way God Works" 97

TWENTY-FIFTH SUNDAY IN ORDINARY TIME
Spanish Springs Presbyterian Church, Sparks, Nevada, September 19, 1999
Exodus 16:2–15; Philippians 1:21–30; Matthew 20:1–16
"God's Economy" 102

TWENTY-SIXTH SUNDAY IN ORDINARY TIME
Spanish Springs Presbyterian Church, Sparks, Nevada, September 25, 2005
Exodus 17:1–7; Philippians 2:1–13; Matthew 21:23–32
"God in Our Wilderness" 108

TWENTY-SEVENTH SUNDAY IN ORDINARY TIME
Spanish Springs Presbyterian Church, Sparks, Nevada, October 2, 2011
Exodus 20:1–4, 7–9, 12–20; Philippians 3:4b–14; Matthew 21:33–46
"Taste, and See" 113

TWENTY-EIGHTH SUNDAY IN ORDINARY TIME
First Presbyterian Church, Ponca City, Oklahoma, October 19, 2014
Exodus 32:1–14; Philippians 1:4–9; Matthew 22:1–14
"God on Our Terms?" 118

TWENTY-NINTH SUNDAY IN ORDINARY TIME
First Presbyterian Church, Norfolk, Nebraska, October 21, 1990
Exodus 33:12–23; 1 Thessalonians 1:1–10; Matthew 22:15–22
"When Faith Comes Alive" 123

THIRTIETH SUNDAY IN ORDINARY TIME
First Presbyterian Church, Dodge City, Kansas, October 27, 1996
Deuteronomy 34:1–12; 1 Thessalonians 2:1–8; Matthew 22:34–42
"Hold Nothing Back" 128

THIRTY-FIRST SUNDAY IN ORDINARY TIME
Spanish Springs Presbyterian Church, Sparks, Nevada, October 31, 1999
Joshua 3:7–17; 1 Thessalonians 2:9–13; Matthew 23:1–12
"What Is a Saint?" 133

ALL SAINTS' DAY
Revelation 7:9–17; 1 John 3:1–3; Matthew 5:1–12
"Of Blessed Memory" 139

THIRTY-SECOND SUNDAY IN ORDINARY TIME
Spanish Springs Presbyterian Church, Sparks, Nevada, November 6, 2005
Joshua 24:1–3a, 14–25; 1 Thessalonians 14:13–18; Matthew 25:1–13
"Pledge of Allegiance" 144

THIRTY-THIRD SUNDAY IN ORDINARY TIME
Spanish Springs Presbyterian Church, Sparks, Nevada, November 17, 2002
Judges 4:1–7; 1 Thessalonians 5:1–11; Matthew 25:14–30
"The Memories in the Closet" 149

CHRIST THE KING
Spanish Springs Presbyterian Church, Sparks, Nevada, November 23, 2008
Ezekiel 34:11–16, 20–24; Ephesians 1:15–23; Matthew 25:31–46
"As If the Pauper Were the Prince" 157

EVENING BEFORE THE NATIONAL DAY OF THANKSGIVING
Spanish Springs Presbyterian Church, Sparks, Nevada, November 26, 2008
Deuteronomy 8:1–10; 2 Corinthians 9:6–15; Matthew 6:25–33
"Keeping the Gift a Blessing"   162

Appendix
TWENTY-NINTH SUNDAY IN ORDINARY TIME
St. John's Presbyterian Church, Reno, Nevada, October 16, 2005
Exodus 33:12–23; 1 Thessalonians 1:1–10; Matthew 22:15–22
"God in the Afterglow"   168

List of Sourced Cited   173

Introduction

OVER THE LENGTH OF human history, people have sought answers to the riddle of why certain things happen to them. Causality and explanation are at the heart of the religious quest, and the Bible, by its very existence, is witness to the universal insistence that the world and its phenomena have meaning and purpose, and to the hope that events in personal and common life have predictability and yield a positive outcome.

The Hebrew scriptures are testimony that God is active in nature and in human affairs. The New Testament inherited that same faith-based assumption. Without ever achieving a consensus about the manner of providence, either in individual instances or within the larger scope of history, nevertheless theologians and everyday believers have seen in the Bible assertive confirmation that, in the words of Arthur Campbell Ainger,

> God is working His purpose out / As year succeeds to year:
> God is working His purpose out, / And the time is drawing near;
> Nearer and nearer draws the time, / The time that shall surely be,
> When the earth shall be filled with the glory of God / As the waters cover the sea.[1]

Writing in the final decade of the nineteenth century, Ainger gave voice to the divine side of what was commonly perceived to be an undeniable progression of human behavior, even human nature, toward perfection of God's purpose of morality, intelligence, and harmony. Scientific advance, coupled with discoveries in psychology and development of the social sciences, seemed, in the minds of many, conclusive proof of the gospel's promised victory over systemic evil. The text of Ainger's hymn goes on to envision an inevitable evangelization of the world that would demonstrate the glory of God unequivocally and irrefutably. God was mightily at work, and human efforts toward improvement of moral, physical, and social conditions, if blessed by God, would follow a course charted in heaven toward an earthly paradise restored.

Events in the first decades of the twentieth century challenged fundamentally that interpretation of God's work within history, as the great age of

---

1. Ainger, "God Is Working His Purpose Out."

progress was shattered on the battlefields of Christian Europe, and a new era of martial brutality, enabled by many of the very discoveries and technologies that had signaled human progress, now resulted in the deaths of millions. In response, the neoorthodox theological movement reaffirmed the stubborn persistence of human sin and human ignorance over any temporary advance toward general human cooperation and human compassion.

Without stating a uniform explanation of the principle, scripture is nevertheless confident about God's purpose and God's power and God's effectiveness, with the exception of sporadic bursts of lament that have traditionally been dismissed as instances of myopic human doubt and misunderstanding. Recent theology and homiletics have been more respectful of skepticism and uncertainty as something other than unfaith and more willing to entertain the possibility that God's power is limited, in expression if not in essence, by feckless human behavior and amoral natural phenomena. This perspective on God's work is affirmed in the Bible itself, where God is shown to be constrained and redirected by human choices and sometimes even by human argument. Yet, for all the myriad qualifications and exceptions that can be cited from personal experience, as well as scriptural record, the eyes of faith insistently detect God present and working in and through the events of individuals, communities, and nations, as well as the ongoing forces of nature, both dramatic and inconspicuous, and toward a goal unfailingly gracious and constant in the heart and mind of God.

As I write this, roughly a century after the Western world's conviction that the worst days were behind it dissolved in the inhumanities of Ypres and Verdun and a hundred other European battlefields, we are witnessing an atrocity in Ukraine that rivals, certainly, the worst moments of World War I or any other barbarity known to history, even the unutterable inhumanities leading up to and during World War II. Orthodox Easter has just been observed in the cathedrals of Moscow and Kyiv and thousands of other places of worship in Russia and Ukraine, marked, according to reports, by prayers for blessings upon the strategists and aggressors in the one nation and the defenders and victims in the other. If God possesses any power at all, if indeed there is a God, how can this new atrocity be happening, with tens of thousands killed and maimed, many of them children, and millions of other innocents displaced, apartment houses leveled and women raped, now in the twenty-first century? Clearly, God does not work, or is not working, by snapping the divine fingers to stop the madness even among people who loudly assert their Christian faith as justification for the most satanic behavior. But the horror and riveted attention of the world to the suffering of the Ukrainians, and the prayers of the outraged that prompt sacrificial deeds of compassion, opening hearts and opening borders and opening doors to the refugees, willing at least to curb otherwise insatiable private profit and convenience to throw a spoke in the wheel of the aggressor's war machine, to borrow from Dietrich Bonhoeffer's imagery—is that not God at work, and powerfully so, in the hearts of people moved by the words and witness of Christ? Even the anguished reluctance to aid in ways that would likely invite more and wider destruction and suffering—perhaps that restraint is God at work, too, though a terrible circumstance of having to choose between the lesser of two undeniable evils.

And so, we must conclude, God works to achieve the great divine purpose, sometimes at least, by infusing the Spirit's testimony to selfless love and cruciform integrity in the hearts of those who witness suffering and sacrifice to put in motion the only available means to remedy or ameliorate it. How many such atrocities have been prevented by the heroic efforts of diplomats and agencies reacting to history's previous atrocities? How many prayers have been offered that humankind will find a better future than its checkered past, sustaining by the power of the Holy Spirit the healers and the peacemakers who provide the hands and feet by which the lordship of Christ is given witness in history's darkest moments? Perhaps even the prayer of a single believer animates God's own hope and conviction that "the earth shall be filled with the glory of God as the waters cover the sea."[2]

As I revisited the sermons included in this collection, preached in various locations and over a career in pastoral ministry, I became aware of a recurrent theme that God is at work in ways subtle and astounding, quiet and dramatic, in human hearts as much as in headlines, and that the truth of that is proclaimed throughout the lectionary readings selected for the liturgical time following Pentecost in the Year A cycle. God's providence must often pursue a circuitous route, accommodating itself to human wickedness, caprice, recalcitrance, and obtuseness. But God, in the unalterable divine resolve that the beloved creation will be redeemed, is more stubborn than all the obstacles and impediments. Sin's pretension will be supplanted by salvation's promise. The defeat of the cross will become the triumph of the resurrection. For, truly, God is at work.

---

2. Ainger, "God Is Working His Purpose Out."

THE DAY OF PENTECOST
First Presbyterian Church, Norfolk, Nebraska
JUNE 3, 1990

Acts 2:1–21
Romans 8:14–17
John 14:8–17, 25–27

"An Experience of Pentecost"

(Text in regular type is spoken by preacher, text in bold type is read by lector, text in upper case is voiced by chorus.)

IT IS THE DAY of Pentecost, the great Jewish festival which comes seven weeks after the Passover, marking the anniversary of God's gift of the law at Sinai, the climactic manifestation of God to his chosen people in deafening sound and dazzling sight. **"On the morning of the third day there was thunder and lightning, as well as a thick cloud on the mountain, and a blast of a trumpet so loud that all the people who were in the camp trembled. Moses brought the people out of the camp to meet God. They took their stand at the foot of the mountain. Now Mount Sinai was wrapped in smoke, because the LORD had descended upon it in fire; the smoke went up like the smoke of a kiln, while the whole mountain shook violently. As the blast of the trumpet grew louder and louder, Moses would speak and God would answer him in thunder"** (Exod 19:16–19). The place is Jerusalem, and great throngs of Jewish pilgrims have come to the holy city from every corner of the earth where Jews live in order to participate in the ritual which looked toward God's future restoration of Israel. And also gathered there in Jerusalem the morning of Pentecost were the followers of Jesus, now feeling bewildered and powerless and alone after Christ's ascension, waiting, watching, and wondering, frightened at the dizzying events that they had witnessed in so short a period of time. There was no spirit within them.

"And suddenly from heaven there came a sound like the rush of a violent wind, and it filled the entire house where they were sitting" (Acts 2:2). WIND. Could it be the same wind which on the very first morning of all mornings swept across the dark water? *A MIGHTY WIND.* Could it be the wind of creation? *THE RUSH OF A MIGHTY WIND.* Could it be the same wind that blew life into the first human being? "In the day that the Lord God made the earth and the heavens, when no plant of the field was yet in the earth and no herb of the field had yet sprung up—for the Lord God had not caused it to rain upon the earth, and there was no one to till the ground; but a stream would rise from the earth, and water the whole face of the ground—then the Lord God formed man from the dust of the ground, and breathed into his nostrils the breath of life; and the man became a living being" (Gen 2:4b–7). Could it be a wind that once again was bringing something to life where there had been no life before? "In the beginning when God created the heavens and the earth, the earth was a formless void and darkness covered the face of the deep, while a wind from God swept over the face of the waters" (1:1–2).

What first had been only *heard*, then was *seen*—tongues as of fire. "As the people were filled with expectation, and all were questioning in their hearts concerning John [the Baptist], whether he might be the Messiah, John answered all of them by saying, 'I baptize you with water; but one who is more powerful than I is coming; I am not worthy to untie the thong of his sandals. He will baptize you with the Holy Spirit and fire'" (Luke 3:15–16). First, tongues as of fire. *TONGUES.* And then different tongues of speech. *A GIFT OF TONGUES.* And the people gathered there in Jerusalem from all corners of the earth each heard the mighty words of God being declared in each one's own native language. *HOW CAN THIS BE?* The disciples were filled with the Holy Spirit and began to speak in other tongues. *ARE THESE NOT GALILEANS?* The same disciples who only moments before were dejected and afraid. *WE HEAR THEM TELLING IN THEIR OWN TONGUES THE MIGHTY WORKS OF GOD.* And all were amazed and perplexed. *WHAT DOES THIS MEAN?*

Notice how Luke shows that already the proclamation of the gospel was drawing people's attention—just the first crowd of many in the book of Acts which gather and hear the proclamation of the good news. *WHAT DOES THIS MEAN?* But as happened whenever the gospel was preached, some heard with interest, some heard with believing hearts, but some mocked. *THEY ARE FILLED WITH NEW WINE.*

Finally, Peter, of all people, stood up and spoke to the crowd—Peter, the uncouth, unlearned, rough, rash fisherman, Peter. *COWARD!* Peter, who, in the hour of his Lord's greatest need and greatest sacrifice, denied Jesus not once, not twice, but three times. **"Then they seized [Jesus] and led him away, bringing him into the high priest's house. But Peter was following at a distance. When they had kindled a fire in the middle of the courtyard and sat down together, Peter sat among them. Then a servant-girl, seeing him in the firelight, stared at him and said, 'This man was also with him.' But he denied it, saying, 'Woman, I do not know him.' A little later someone else, on seeing him, said, 'You also are one of them.' But Peter said, 'Man, I am not!' Then about an hour later still another kept insisting, 'Surely this man also was with him; for he is a Galilean.' But Peter said, 'Man, I do not know what you are talking about!' At that moment, while he was still speaking, the cock crowed. The Lord turned and looked at Peter. Then Peter remembered the word of the Lord, how he had said to him, 'Before the cock crows today, you will deny me three times.' And he went out and wept bitterly"** (22:54–62). See whom the Holy Spirit had now brought back to life! Peter, of all people, speaking boldly in defense of the disciples and proclaiming the gospel of the Lord! **"In the last days it will be, God declares, that I will pour out my Spirit upon all flesh, and your sons and your daughters shall prophesy, and your young men shall see visions, and your old men shall dream dreams. . . . Then everyone who calls on the name of the Lord shall be saved"** (Acts 2:17, 21). Ordinary, bumbling, thick-headed Peter. *THE GIFT OF TONGUES.* Here is an eloquence and an urgency which he had never possessed prior to that Pentecost morning—new life, new perception, new reservoirs of strength which had not been in this Galilean fisherman before. *TONGUES AS OF FIRE.* And so did the other disciples find themselves speaking out boldly, performing miracles of preaching and teaching, and carrying the gospel to the ends of the earth in the face of every danger of travel and every threat of persecution. *WHAT DOES THIS MEAN?*

The book of Acts was written for a church that was struggling to maintain its boldness, confidence, and faith while waiting for Christ's return. It was written in a time of persecution and self-doubt, of skepticism and despair. As Luke remembered the words that Jesus spoke when he prepared to take leave of the disciples, and as Luke reflected upon the experience of the church receiving the Holy Spirit, he began to understand more and more the ministry of the church and the power with which that ministry can be accomplished. And the book of Acts which he wrote *called* and *still* calls the church to remember that the power of the Holy Spirit is the power to witness to the mighty acts of God in Jesus Christ, to recognize that the preaching and doing of the gospel depends not upon human resources alone. **"I will pour out my Spirit"** (2:17).

By ourselves, we cannot do the work that we have been given to do, any more than Peter and the other disciples could do, huddled despondent in the upper room. But we are given the Holy Spirit—something of Christ's own ways and mind and nature—to bring all things spiritual within our reach. Ordinary people, once Christ's Spirit has touched and inspired and quickened them, *can* live and *do* live, *can* serve and *do* serve God, as they could *not* do before. SO GOD CREATED HUMANKIND IN HIS OWN IMAGE, IN THE IMAGE OF GOD HE CREATED THEM. It is the Holy Spirit that empowers ordinary people like you and me to do extraordinary things through the church, to perform miracles of restoring the broken to wholeness, of binding up festering wounds, of reconciling those who are divided by hatred and pride, of proclaiming the good news of Jesus Christ in words of hope and deeds of courage. **"And your sons and your daughters shall prophesy, and your young men shall see visions, and your old men shall dream dreams"** (2:17). It is the Holy Spirit that drives the church into every land, serving and pouring itself out in Christ's name for the sake of the world that God loves. It is through the Holy Spirit that the mission of God's people to all the nations is fulfilled. So God manifests himself in the last days. *GOD KEEPS HIS PROMISES.* And it is to the church that God has given this gift. *LIKE THE RUSH OF A WIND.* Even to First Presbyterian Church. *A MIGHTY WIND.*

Trinity Sunday

First Presbyterian Church, Norfolk, Nebraska

June 10, 1990

Deuteronomy 4:32–40
2 Corinthians 13:5–14
Matthew 28:16–20

"Experiencing the Faith"

Paul Achtemeier, professor of New Testament at Union Theological Seminary in Richmond, Virginia, has pointed out that the Bible is, among other things, a confession of faith of the people of God.[1] The Bible sets forth the experience and reflection of a community of believing people over a period of hundreds of years—the experience of its encounters with God and its reflections upon the meaning of those encounters. It sets forth a truth which is more intuited than reasoned, more felt than demonstrable, more experienced than explained. As such, the Bible is of supreme importance to us. We believe that its writers were divinely inspired in their work. Yet, they were human, and they were bound of necessity to the perceptions of the human senses and the understandings of the human mind, to the categories of human thought and the limitations of human expression. At times, they must have groped for human words capable of giving witness to what is ultimately a divine mystery. Frequently, they found their minds inadequate to the task of measuring the power of God. But, always, they felt compelled to set forth for generations yet unborn the faithfulness of God as God's people had experienced it.

In our time, some people are prone to worship the Bible, to forget that the *written* Word is not an end in itself, but rather a sign which points to the *living* Word. Many modern Christians seem to interpret the Bible more

---

1. See, generally, Achtemeier, *Inspiration of Scripture*, and esp. 90–91, 115, 117.

as an encyclopedia of divine moralisms than as a dynamic witness to God's purpose of redeeming his beloved creation. So it is useful to remind ourselves from time to time of the experiential and confessional nature of the scriptures—that they are a uniquely authoritative expression of faith, but one which grew out of theological reflection upon the living experience of the people of God. That reflection disclosed more and more over time the nature of God and God's purpose for creation. One of the best examples of this is scripture's testimony that the God of Abraham and Sarah, of Ruth and David, is the God who creates, redeems, and sustains. The Bible is an unequivocal witness to the truth that God has created everything there is for his own purpose, that God has acted in history to save his people from the effects of their own alienation from him, and that God has supported his people in their journey toward the life which he intends for them. All this, the people of God had experienced in their own history.

Evidence suggests that the book of Deuteronomy in its final form comes from the period of the Babylonian exile and was written for a people who were feeling disinherited by God and who wondered whether the ancient covenant between God and God's people had come to an end. The book rests on much older material, of course, that is expressed for the most part as a long speech by Moses to the people of Israel just before they entered the promised land. But the *concern* of the book, the theological *message* of the book, relates directly to the doubts that were being voiced by a despondent people living in exile away from the promised land many centuries *after* Moses. In *answer* to their anxiety, our reading this morning serves to remind dispirited people of *every* age of the God who created humankind, the God who spoke from a burning bush, the God who claimed his chosen people from bondage in the midst of Egypt, the God who led them into Canaan and drove out its inhabitants so that his people might have a home in the world. "So acknowledge today and take to heart that the LORD is God in heaven above and on the earth beneath; there is no other. Keep his statutes and his commandments, which I am commanding you today for your own well-being and that of your descendants after you, so that you may long remain in the land that the LORD your God is giving you for all time" (Deut 4:39–40). Scripture witnesses to the God who *creates*, who *redeems*, and who *sustains*, and the speech of Moses here summons the people to remember that their God is the one true God who does all of these things—that their faith is based on long experience of God's faithfulness and God's grace.

It is perhaps a habit of human nature, shared across the centuries, that we so quickly seek to reduce experience to a formula, to suppose that truth can be *packaged* and *studied* and *taught*, *better* than it can be *seen* and *touched* and *tasted*. From a very early time, at least from the days that the apostles first took the Christian faith into the cities and countryside of the Greek and Roman world, there was a premium placed on what one *thought* about Jesus Christ. At one point in the early days of the church, faith became so much an intellectual exercise that many Christians came to believe that one's salvation results from having secret knowledge imparted by Christ to the spiritually elite. Do you understand the implications of such a belief? Were that *so*, our salvation would *not* be so much a result of Christ's crucifixion and resurrection, as a product of intellectual insight bestowed upon the chosen few. The church promptly recognized the hazard of such an approach, and branded such teaching as heresy, but it remains with us today, alive and well, stronger perhaps since the days of the Enlightenment than ever before. It plagues Protestantism especially, and has resulted in both spiritual apathy within the mainline churches and an idolizing of doctrine within Fundamentalism. It causes us to assume that the faith has more to do with *right creeds* than *obedient actions*. It tempts us to think that we can be God's people in *isolation*, supposing that salvation is purely a matter of personal belief. It leads us to conceive of evangelism as bringing people into conformity with our modes of expression, as if the task of making disciples were primarily the process of tutoring converts to memorize and recite doctrine.

Paul was continually distressed at the gap between what the Gentile converts had been taught about Jesus Christ and the manner in which they behaved. The Corinthians, especially, acted contrary to the way of Christ, quarreling, asserting privilege, championing their various teachers. When Paul wrote to the Corinthian church instructing the Christians there to examine themselves, to see whether they were holding to their faith, he was not telling them to compare details of doctrine, but to see that their attitudes and behavior were such as Christ would approve. "Test yourselves," he commanded. "Do you not realize that Jesus Christ is in you?" (2 Cor 13:5). Being a person of God is not simply a matter of knowing what the Bible says and being able to recite the creeds. The Corinthians were far from the community of believers inaugurated by Christ. People in whom Christ dwells are not contentious and factious; they do not point fingers and wag their tongues, finding fault with each other at every opportunity; they do not excuse their immoralities with every sort of rationalization; they do not tear down or create division by complaining of this and that. People in whom Christ dwells seek harmony with each other and look for every opportunity to make peace; they encourage and show gratitude toward each other; they pattern their conduct on the humility and compassion and servanthood of Christ; they work to heal and build up, and to glorify God.

For the earliest Christians, of course, there were no theological doctrines. There was teaching, certainly—the Gospels declare over and over that Jesus taught his disciples, helping them to reflect upon the Jewish scriptures and upon their own experience, helping them to perceive how God was presently active in their own time, in their own lives and most of all in the world around them. There were no elaborate Christian treatises—in fact, there was not even a New Testament as we know it—but some shared remembrances of what Jesus said and did, supplemented by brief hymns and creeds and simple catechisms and the testimony of the apostles, all of which expressed their common faith. What there was, mostly, was an abiding sense of the presence of Christ—an experience of God present with them and at work in and through them that confirmed what Jesus had said, producing miracles which they believed could never have occurred had their Lord not been raised from the dead and been exalted to a heavenly throne, and had he not sent the Holy Spirit among them.

This is Trinity Sunday, a day first designated about a thousand years ago to focus the attention of the church upon a doctrine which has become central to the Christian faith—a theologically complex teaching first formulated at the Council of Nicaea in the year 325. But we do not celebrate the doctrine, the expression of a divine fact in poor human words, so much as we give thanks for the mystery behind the doctrine. For most of us, the concept of the Trinity seems so fundamental to Christianity and so implicit in the New Testament scripture that it surprises us to realize that the word "Trinity" appears nowhere in the Bible. As a doctrine, it came into existence only after long reflection by the early generations of Christians—reflection about the God of the law and the prophets, reflection about the testimony to the words and deeds of Jesus, both before and after the crucifixion, and reflection about their experience of Christ alive and at work within their community, changing human hearts and empowering for discipleship and producing miracle after miracle. The doctrine of the Trinity is an attempt to define in human language a truth far beyond human conception, and yet a truth that was absolute in its reality for the early Christians and *remains* absolute in its reality for Christians around the world today—a truth experienced daily by all people who have discovered in God the very one who created all that is and continues to be the creative Father, the very one who brought his people up out of bondage and enslavement and continues, through the Son, to free people from sin and fear and pride and oppression, and the very one who spoke to Moses out of a burning bush and gave the prophets courage to speak words of judgment to the corrupt and words of comfort to the afflicted and *continues* to inspire and empower and nurture his people through the Holy Spirit.

The Gospel of Matthew proclaims the appearance of the risen Lord to the remaining eleven disciples on a mountain in Galilee, telling us that "when they saw him they worshiped him; but some doubted" (Matt 28:17). Jesus, they knew. But the doctrine of the resurrection was completely new to them. Jesus spoke to his followers about God being his Father, and he promised them the Holy Spirit. But the doctrine of the Trinity was centuries away. Their faith was based upon what they had experienced—the historic faithfulness of the God of the law and the prophets to his people Israel; their friend Jesus, who preached and taught and healed as one with divine authority and who died on a cross but then was raised from the dead and appeared to them and ate with them; and finally an abiding sense of Christ's presence and the fullness of God with them even after Christ's ascension, an indwelling divinity that comforted and encouraged and empowered. The community of believers reflected upon this experience and remembered the words of the Old Testament scriptures and the words and actions of their Lord and his promise of the Spirit. And as they did so, they came to discern the marvelous and mysterious truth which is God, three persons but one divine substance, Creator, Redeemer, and Sustainer—Father, Son, and Holy Spirit—God not only ruling the universe, but living in each believer; God not only judging, but saving; God not only revealing his will on tablets of stone, but in innocent blood shed from a cross; God not only parting the seas, but brightening a care-worn face with a smile; God not only speaking in thundering clouds, but whispering in the human heart. And they perceived that all things were possible with such a God as they had experienced—even going and making disciples of all nations, doers of God's will of redeeming his beloved creation—baptizing them into eternal life and incomparable joy, teaching them to do all the things that Jesus had commanded his *first* disciples to do.

And they did it! And the church does it still. "The great ends of the Church," as the Constitution of the Presbyterian Church declares, "are the proclamation of the Gospel for the salvation of humankind; the shelter, nurture and spiritual fellowship of the children of God; the maintenance of divine worship; the preservation of the truth; the promotion of social righteousness; and the exhibition of the Kingdom of Heaven to the world."[2] The church exists not so that these things of the faith can be formulated into doctrines of human words, although that certainly is a significant by-product. The church exists for the *doing* of all of these things of faith, so that every man, woman, and child experiences the same love that Jesus Christ showed. And when the faith is *not* experienced in that way in the church—when

---

2. *Book of Order*, F-1.0304.

there is discord and complaint and division and self-assertion—then the words of Paul ring out anew across the breadth of the Christian era: "Do you not realize that Jesus Christ is in you? . . . Put things in order, listen to my appeal, agree with one another, live in peace; and the God of love and peace will be with you" (2 Cor 13:5, 11).

We have been given all that we need to fulfill our commission from our Lord—all the love and power and inspiration required to go and make disciples of all nations, baptizing them in the name of the Father and of the Son and of the Holy Spirit, teaching them to observe all that Christ commanded. And in the very last words of the Good News according to Matthew, we have Jesus' own promise that keeps all of this from becoming mere human words and lifeless propositions, Jesus' own promise that calls us to venture out of our books and our creeds, and invites us to *experience* what our formulas of doctrine can only *hint* at: "And remember, I am with you always, to the end of the age" (Matt 28:20b).

Eighth Sunday in Ordinary Time
Spanish Springs Presbyterian Church, Sparks, Nevada
May 25, 2008

Isaiah 49:8–16a
1 Corinthians 4:1–5
Matthew 6:24–34

"Consider the Lilies"

"Dad," Lucas Macleod said after the insurance agent had left the office and closed the door behind him, "that's an awful lot of money. Surely there's a better use for it than insuring the warehouse for the full sales value of a full inventory. For that matter, when was the last time that the warehouse was anywhere *near* full? It's mainly empty space. It's highly unlikely that there will *ever* be an actual loss in the amount that you're *paying* for."

"And what if something happens that one day that it *is* full, Lucas?" Walter Macleod shook his head. "We'd be out hundreds of thousands."

"We wouldn't be *out* hundreds of thousands. We simply wouldn't *make* hundreds of thousands," the younger man said. "That money you're planning to spend could be used in a lot better ways."

"Like *what*?" the older man demanded in an irritated voice. "What could be a better expenditure than securing our investment?"

"Dad, when was the last time we gave our people a raise?"

"What's *that* got to do with it?"

"*They're* the people who keep us in *business*. They've been loyal to us—to *you*—for many years, most of them. And they haven't had an increase in five years."

"And I haven't given *myself* a raise. All of our profits go back into the business. I'm securing *their* future as much as *mine*—as much as yours, and Melinda's!"

"No, Dad. You're *jeopardizing* their future under the pretext of guaranteeing it. They're falling behind. And with today's increases in gasoline and groceries and just about everything else, those who aren't *already* hurting are *going* to be."

The older man scowled at his son. "I'm busy," he grumbled, turning his swivel chair away from the younger man. "I've got things I have to do before the graduation."

"Dad, I don't mean to upset you. I don't like to contradict you. But it's not fair to these people who work their hearts out for us."

"I'm not robbing them of anything," the older man snapped, still with his back turned to his son. "They're not getting anything less than they contracted for. And *I* don't take home much more than *they* do."

Lucas sighed, and his eyes happened to fall on a new item sitting on his father's credenza. It was a picture frame, about five inches by seven, that held an engraved invitation. Lucas knew without reading it what the invitation said, but he was a little surprised, as well as pleased, to see it so ennobled with pride of place in his father's office.

"I see you framed Melinda's graduation invitation. That was a nice thing to do."

"I have another frame for the announcement, when she sends them out after graduation," the older man said, his voice now considerably gentler than when he had been arguing with his son. Lucas could see him bend his head forward as he added, "I wish that your mother . . . ." But he didn't finish the sentence.

"So do I," Lucas said after several seconds. "She would have been very proud."

"She means everything to me," the older man said, still facing away from his son and his voice choking slightly. "She has been such a perfect angel—kind, loving."

Alongside the framed invitation on the top of his credenza were half a dozen framed photographs of his granddaughter—his only grandchild—at different ages, and a somewhat faded photograph of himself and his late wife and Lucas, then only a teenager. "And now, the first in our family to graduate from university. Just imagine! Where have the years gone?"

Lucas looked through the window at the complex of buildings that housed the family business on the outskirts of Oakville—a small factory, run by about two dozen employees, most of them now middle-aged or older who had been with Macleod Industries all their working lives, and a couple of *their* children just starting their working lives but promising to be good craftsmen someday, and the warehouse that, as soon as Walter Macleod signed the binder, would be insured for full replacement value plus the wholesale value of up to two thousand items of furniture, though the chairs, tables, and cabinets were in such demand, and took so long to craft, that the warehouse was seldom as much as a third full. Furniture dealers across the country knew them to be well-made from quality wood, more expensive than what was carried in the chain stores but still an outstanding value.

Walter Macleod had been apprenticed to a carpenter in his youth in Smiths Falls, and had shown such skill and aptitude with wood that he had soon come down to the city to open his own shop. There, he had met and married his darling Madeline, and they had had one child—Lucas—who was destined from the crib to be his father's business partner. It had been a source of embarrassment to Walter that he himself had never finished high school. Others might have envied him his success, but Walter always felt that his accomplishments were tarnished by his decision to leave school as soon as he was able. He and Madeline had hoped that Lucas might have a fine education, but his business had expanded so rapidly that he pressed his son to join him in the office after Lucas had had only one year of university, and he sometimes felt that he had cheated his son. The younger Macleod was personable and smart, and would have done well at anything he had chosen to do. Perhaps it was to make up for that that Walter had insisted on paying for Melinda's education. It had been a bit of a strain, financially, but he had been determined to do it. Not that he had ever spent a great deal of time with his granddaughter, though she was often the subject of his conversation. When he *had* been with her, he had given her his full attention, including a rare multigenerational vacation to Disney World when the girl was only six. His wife, bless her, had doted on the child, sometimes to the point of disapproval by their son and daughter-in-law. Madeline's death had left a big hole in all of their lives, and Walter had seemed to turn even more to his business, arriving at the office by 7:00 a.m. and working often until ten or eleven at night, telephoning suppliers, writing to customers, personally inspecting the finished pieces for quality before allowing them to be shipped, but never forgetting his granddaughter's birthday or other special occasions, and always eager to hear news of her life and always eager, with pride, to tell others of her accomplishments. Quite simply, Melinda was the apple of his eye. She was an above-average student, not exceptional, but, as far as he was concerned, no student would ever be more deserving of a diploma when they all walked across the stage that afternoon.

"I think we should leave shortly," Lucas said.

"Yes, certainly," his father answered, turning the chair around, revealing eyes that were red as he pulled a handkerchief from his pocket and wiped them and then blew his nose. "I've been looking forward to this."

There was a knock on the door.

"Come in," Walter Macleod said.

The door opened to reveal Anna Jenkins, his efficient and dedicated sixty-something-year-old secretary who had a look of extreme worry on her face. "I'm sorry to interrupt you, Mr. Walter," she said, utilizing the customary form of address that the employees used to distinguish the older man from his son. "Mr. Lucas," she nodded in acknowledgment that the younger man, too, was being interrupted.

"That's fine, Anna," the older man said. "Is something wrong?"

"Hugh Mitchell, the factory foreman, just called. There's been a mishap."

"What happened?" Walter Macleod barked, rising quickly to his feet.

"Is anybody hurt?" Lucas Macleod asked, his face a study in apprehension.

"No, fortunately. Just wet, I take it. The fire sprinklers in the upholstery shop went off—"

"There's been a fire?" the older man broke in to her explanation.

"No, no. The system was being inspected, and somehow the sprinklers went off by accident. No one was hurt, but all the upholstered chairs in the shop have been damaged."

The two men bolted past the secretary and ran through the office building and toward the factory. When they arrived, not quite breathless, at the upholstery shop, Hugh Mitchell was complaining loudly to a man dressed in a workman's uniform that had the words "Fire Men, Incorporated" embroidered on the shirt. The entire floor was wet, and scores of dining room chairs, each with upholstered seats, dripped rust-colored water. When the foreman saw his bosses, he broke off his tirade and became all apology.

"I'm so sorry, Mr. Walter, Mr. Lucas. It was just the regular inspection of the fire suppression system, and . . . ." There was really no need to continue. The results of the exercise were obvious all around them.

"Bad valve," the uniformed man muttered, looking at his feet.

"Well, we can't undo what happened," said Lucas Macleod. "Can the woodwork be salvaged?"

"I think so," said the foreman. Already, a brigade of workers had appeared, armed with towels. "If we get to them right away, it shouldn't damage the finish. The problem is the fabric. It's ruined, of course, and I know you wouldn't want to send out anything that wasn't absolutely right. And this lot was all scheduled to be shipped tomorrow to Nelson's—that new account in Windsor. We were already running a week behind on it," he shook his head in frustration, "because that caning shipment arrived late."

"We've got to get that shipment out. I'll help you," Walter Macleod said, starting to roll up his sleeves. "Do you need me cutting? Stapling? What?"

"Dad! The graduation!"

"But son, this is business. We can't risk losing Nelson's. They're the finest furniture store in that whole region. It was quite a plum getting this order—a major foot in the door. I worked *months* to win that account—so did *you*. You were down there half a dozen times. You go on to the graduation and tell Melinda how sorry I am. Then come back as soon as you can."

"Dad, no." Lucas Macleod turned to the foreman with a pleading look. "This is the biggest day in Melinda's life," he explained. The foreman was at a loss, reluctant to contradict the owner of the company. Lucas turned back to his father. "It's one of the biggest days in *your* life, too. So there's a delay of a few more days—"

"But son! Nelson's!"

"They'll just have to understand. And if they don't, we'll find another account."

Hugh Mitchell finally spoke. "Mr. Walter, there's not a person on the payroll who won't work around the clock to get these chairs redone and shipped out as fast as possible. Shouldn't you be there when Melinda walks across the stage? There's hundreds of furniture stores, Mr. Walter, but you only have one granddaughter."

As he said this, Anna Jenkins, the secretary, joined the group of men. "Can I help, Mr. Walter?" she asked. "I changed my shoes," she said, pointing to the tennis shoes on her feet which had replaced her customary high heels. She looked a model of incongruity, clothed in a prim pink office dress and sneakers.

Lucas Macleod could not help bursting out in laughter, which caused the secretary to go red with an embarrassed self-consciousness. "Miss Jenkins," he said, embracing her, "you are a gem."

Still embarrassed when he released her, she strove to recover her normal decorum. "Shouldn't you be getting on to the graduation, Mr. Lucas, Mr. Walter?"

By now, the other employees of Macleod Industries were carrying the chairs out of the upholstery shop to where they could be dried off thoroughly and the old fabric and foam rubber removed. Pete Lawson ran in to the shop, also armed with a towel. "Mr. Mitchell," he said, "I called the fabric supplier, and they can have the same patterns here by tomorrow. They said they'd bend over backwards to help us. Good thing we ran late on getting the caning—they said last week the whole place was shut down because of some mechanical problems, and the staff was all given an unexpected holiday!"

"Come on, Dad," Lucas Macleod said, pulling at his father's elbow. "We don't want to be late."

"I . . . I want you to know," the older man said, looking over his shoulder as his son guided him toward the door, "that you're all getting a raise next week. You're the finest . . . you're the best . . . ."

Hundreds of folding chairs were lined up in rows on the grassy expanse of Queen's Park. As soon as they had located three empty seats together as close as possible to the front, Walter Macleod and his son and daughter-in-law had found Melinda's name in the printed program. "With honors," Mrs. Macleod sighed as she read the description. Walter Macleod pursed his lips and gave a little nod to himself as he read the same words. Then he sniffed and looked up toward the stage.

During the thirty minutes or so that preceded the start of the ceremony, the three commented on the weather—which was pleasant, fortunately—and on the dress of the people who passed to their right or left, finding seats—Walter Macleod was in his very finest suit—and on the birds singing in the trees, still audible above the din of the gathering families and friends of the graduates, and on the flower arrangements on the stage. "They're too far away," Lucas Macleod said when his wife drew attention to them. "I can't see what they are."

"Lilies, I think," she answered.

"That's nice, isn't it?" Walter Macleod observed in a general mood of approbation. "That's nice," he repeated. Then he said, changing the subject, "I hope I made the dinner reservations for the right time." Months before, he had announced that he wanted to take the graduate and her parents to dinner, following graduation, at the big stately hotel that had been an emblem of the city for so long, and that had so impressed him when he and his wife had first moved there. He had taken Madeline there for their anniversary once—a practice he would like to have made into a habit, but, whenever their anniversary approached, it had seemed an extravagance beyond the means of their modest lifestyle. On this occasion, however, nothing was too good. It seemed the natural thing to do.

Then, Walter Macleod began to fidget. "I hope everything's going all right at the shop," he said, looking straight ahead but intending for Lucas to hear.

"I'm sure it is, Dad. Everybody's pitching in."

"Well," the older man said, but did not finish the sentence.

At last, the ceremony began. Music was played. Introductions were made. Speeches were given. And the graduates finally walked across the stage, shook hands, and received the cards which indicated their entitlement to their diplomas, which they would actually receive by mail once their final grades were computed. It had been announced, before the parade of graduates across the stage had begun, that some of the students had voluntarily entered an essay contest on the meaning of "success in life," and that the winning essay would be presented by the student who had written it at the point in the ceremony that that person's graduation was recognized. By the time the name "Edward Lunt" was announced, the Macleods were all three on the edge of their seats. Lucas's wife looked at the program and said, "Five to go."

Finally, Melinda Macleod appeared at the right side of the stage as her name was read, along with the words "with honors." Walter Macleod could scarcely contain himself. Tears welled up in the eyes of all three, and actually trickled down the cheeks of Lucas's wife. Then came the announcement from the dean who was reading that set of names, "And Melinda Macleod will now read her winning essay on the meaning of success in life."

"Oh!" Mrs. Macleod said, raising her hand to her lips. "She didn't tell us about this!"

It took a few seconds for Walter and Lucas to comprehend what was happening—to make the connection with the earlier, and by now almost forgotten, announcement regarding the essay contest.

Melinda, with conspicuous poise, approached the podium and cleared her throat. "Ladies and gentlemen," she began, "administrators, faculty, staff, fellow graduates, families, and friends: There is only one true measure of success in life. It is not money. It is not fame. It is not appearance. It is not even health. It is, quite simply, love. And it is not even to *be* loved. It is *to* love—to love others. Some of us have been quite fortunate to know someone who has lived a life of success, so defined. And some of us have been fortunate to receive lessons from that person that are far more important than anything we can have learned from books and lectures." Melinda paused and cleared her throat again. "Let me tell you about my grandfather," she said.

Ninth Sunday in Ordinary Time
Spanish Springs Presbyterian Church, Sparks, Nevada
June 1, 2008

Genesis 6:9–22; 7:24; 8:14–19
Romans 1:16–17; 3:21–31
Matthew 7:21–29

"The Stubborn Creator"

"No more floods," the teenager said. "Next time, fire!" I have heard such predictions of doom from the lips of several people in recent years, fueled perhaps by the type of thinking exhibited in the "Left Behind" series of novels, but I was particularly grieved to hear it one day from a high-school aged girl emerging from a self-styled Christian youth event, and the fact that she was smiling—smirking, even—when she said it. What are some ministers and youth leaders *doing* in the name of Jesus Christ, to convince young people that God is going to destroy the earth with fire, and to encourage them to be gleeful at the prospect of *anyone* being consumed by the flames?

People, we have a job to do—*you* have a job to do, not just the minister—to understand what the Bible *says* and what it *doesn't* say, and to call to account *anyone* who makes reckless misrepresentations of the gospel. If even *half* of the girl's message were correct—that God intends to incinerate the earth—what manner of disciple of Jesus Christ would be *joyous* about it? First of all, what makes anyone so convinced that he or she would be *spared* such punishment? (We're *all* sinners, and we're *all* unrepentant about *something*.) And secondly, Jesus *wept* over Jerusalem and its unrighteous rejection of his ministry, he didn't rub his hands in joyful anticipation of its demise. Why would any true follower of Jesus *smile* at the thought of even the most *notorious* sinner perishing? The fact that it is *churches* that *preach* such unscriptural rubbish, and indoctrinate their youth in such vindictive ways of thinking, that seem to be the fastest-growing, would suggest that they have found a market by tapping in to some all-too-human emotions and motivations, but unworthy ones—the very sorts of attitudes that Jesus came to *reverse*, not to *perpetuate*, and *certainly* not to *hallow*.

One of the few stories in the Bible that nearly everyone knows something about is also one of the most misunderstood. People are very clear about the flood. People are not so clear about the rainbow. And I suspect that *more* people—even more *Christians*—when they see or hear a reference to the ark, think about *destruction* than *salvation*.

Anybody who had eyes to see and ears to hear and a mind to perceive could have *joined* Noah in building an ark back in the days before the flood. The fact that, according to Genesis, it was Noah *alone* who prepared for the days of downpour from the sky and fountains from the deep confirms that he was, indeed, unique in righteousness among his generation. That does not mean that Noah was *sinless*, by the way, nor the *other* members of his family—Christians reserve *that* claim only for *Jesus* and, besides, the Ten Commandments and all the other laws of Moses did not yet exist, so violating *them*, specifically, cannot yet have been a conscious trespass against God. It means that Noah was in a right *relationship* with God, sinner though he undoubtedly was. He acknowledged that it was *God* who had given him life, and so he *worshiped* God, and worshiped *only* God. He was a person of high integrity, and had a close association with God, one of trust and obedience.

God announced to Noah that God was "going to bring a flood of waters on the earth, to destroy from under heaven all flesh in which is the breath of life; everything that is on the earth shall die" (Gen 6:17). And yet, in the very next sentence, God makes it clear that in fact not all flesh *is* going to die. "But I will establish my covenant with you; and you shall come into the ark, you, your sons, your wife, and your sons' wives with you. And of every living thing, of all flesh, you shall bring two of every kind into the ark to keep them alive with you" (6:18–19).

It might be more accurate to say that God did not plan so much to *send* a flood to destroy the surface of the earth and all its creatures, but that God was going to let go the forces of chaos that he had held at bay from the beginning of creation when he separated the waters that were under the dome from the waters that were above the dome—to let the earth experience what life *without* God would be like. The result of the inundation would not be a total *destruction*, but a total *cleansing*. The earth remained. Noah and his family remained. Two creatures of every kind, male and female, remained. It would be a new *start*, but it would be the same *creation*; God had not given up on the world, certainly had no desire to smash it to bits or burn it to a cinder. And God realized that since he could not bring himself to destroy it, the same forces of pride and greed and lust and hatred that had spoiled God's dream the first time around would reassert themselves in the hearts of human beings, would still envelop all creation, including all the other sorts of creatures, in the effects of human sin. But when the waters eventually subsided, God vowed never again to permit the forces of chaos to destroy all flesh. "I will never again curse the ground because of humankind," God said to himself, "for the inclination of the human heart is evil from youth"—God was not willing to put an end to humankind just because of its evil inclinations, nor, apparently, was God willing to take away the free will that *was* and *is* part and parcel of being human—"nor will I ever again destroy every living creature as I have done" (8:21). God remembered that he was, after all, a creator, not a destroyer, an orderer, not an anarchist, a God of love, not a God of revenge. "As long as the earth endures, seedtime and harvest, cold and heat, summer and winter, day and night, shall not cease" (8:22).

God *could* have been like the frustrated artist who, when the painting isn't turning out right, slashes the canvas in disgust and throws it away. That, I guess, is what that high school girl thought was going to happen, or *hoped* was going to happen. And if the world were only a painting, it would make no real difference. Paint on a canvas may represent an idea, but it remains only a depiction, not the real thing—not real beings, not even real grass and trees. When such an experiment goes awry, nothing important is lost by discarding the failure. But when real lives are at stake, living, breathing beings, some of them made in God's own image, could God toss it onto the rubbish heap, or cast it into the incinerator? Not the God testified to in the Bible. The promise of scripture is not a world *replaced*, but a world *transformed*. Creation will *not* ultimately be dashed to bits. It will become the kingdom of God. God does not consider the world and its creatures expendable. God values the world as the very place where the drama of salvation is being accomplished. The story of the ark, and the flood, and the bow in the clouds, is not a tale about a tyrant executing vengeance, but about a parent exercising love.

When a baby is born, adult hearts melt, and no hope for that child, no dream, seems too fantastic. Most parents, though, expect love in return for their love, obedience in return for well-intentioned rules, trust in return for being trustworthy. In time, however, it becomes clear that the child is developing a will of his or her own, not always in harmony with ours. The "terrible twos," in most instances, are appropriately named. A few years later, we deal with adolescence. For some unfortunate parents, that can be a time of heartbreak.

We must walk a fine line between setting few boundaries and enforcing none, and being overly strict or overprotective. It is a matter of "risk." We wring our hands when they go out on a first overnight, on a first date, on a first drive, on a first job. In a new and more dangerous culture, we wring our hands when they go on the internet, even, perhaps, when they go to school. But "go" they must, or be something less than human. And along the way, we learn that they are not perfect, and not carbon copies of ourselves even though they bear something of our image, genetically, in the case of biological parents, attitudinally, in nearly all cases. And that is when we learn better what love means—love for our children not as we *wish* they were, but love for our children as they *are*; love for our children not just when they do what we *think* they should do, but love for our children when they do what they *want* to do; love for our children not just when they *please* us, but, more importantly, love for our children even when they do something that *dis*pleases us and causes us deep anguish.

We have to *learn* to be parents. In spite of parenting classes and parenting books and parenting videos, it can't happen, really, until we *have* children, and now and then become exasperated by them, and determine that our love for them must be unconditional, even as we try to set a good example and impart to them whatever wisdom we have accumulated. I think it is no sacrilege to say that God must have had to learn to be a parent. The book of Genesis indicates that it was during the incident of the flood, after God had been grieved to the heart, that God determined that divine love must also be unconditional, and that he would never destroy, but would work to redeem, the world that he created, and those of its inhabitants who bear, each one of them, something of his image.

The story of the flood and the ark and the rainbow is *not* a definitive *assessment* of the world that God created. It *is* a definitive *affirmation* about God and God's way with the world that he created. It reveals the imposing *power* of God. But it also reveals the stubborn *purpose* of God. It tells of God's *will* for creation, and it also tells of God's *commitment* to creation. God will not forget his expectation for the world that he brought into being, but neither will God abandon all hope for the world by obliterating it or turning his back on it. It remains the object of his hope, even if its inhabitants often cause him heartache. God will not allow himself to give in to anger, but will continue to be the very definition of love. God is not a vengeful tyrant, but a troubled parent, who grieves over every instance of alienation from his children, who feels each of their hurts as if they were his own, who can't stop loving his children even, and especially, when they seem determined to be *un*lovable. This is a God loving and wise enough to discipline but not to coerce. This is a God determined and resolute enough to endure detours but not to give up. This is a God stubborn and patient enough to take pride and joy in what is not yet perfect but never to quit nudging creation toward its full potential and inevitable destination.

    I rather think that God was horrified by what almost happened in this story but didn't quite—the destruction of everything that God had hoped for when he first determined to make a universe, to fashion a world. "Then God said to Noah and to his sons with him, 'As for me, I am establishing my covenant with you and your descendants after you, and with every living creature that is with you, the birds, the domestic animals, and every animal of the earth with you, as many as came out of the ark. I establish my covenant with you, that never again shall all flesh be cut off by the waters of a flood, and never again shall there be a flood to destroy the earth'" (9:8–11). And God set a bow in the clouds as a reminder, whenever the rain started, that it would be meant as a blessing and not a curse, something to make the land fruitful, not to devastate it. Floods there might be, but they would be a fact of nature not yet perfect, *not* a sign that God was not yet merciful. And as with water, so with fire or earthquake or wind or anything else. God is a loving parent who cannot stop loving his children, a stubborn Creator who will not give up on the creation he has begun.

Tenth Sunday in Ordinary Time
Spanish Springs Presbyterian Church, Sparks, Nevada
June 6, 1999

Genesis 12:1–9
Romans 4:13–25
Matthew 9:9–13, 18–26

"Grace at the Table"

In ancient times, perhaps even more than today, the individuals you chose as your companions said a lot about who you were. People judged each other by the company they kept, especially whom they ate with. Our very words "company" and "companion" are made up from the Latin words "with" and "bread"—a "companion" is a person with whom you eat bread. A "company" is literally a group of people who dine together.

In our much more casual culture with hurried lunch hours, or lunch half-hours, we may still prefer to eat with our friends, but other people are less likely to draw conclusions about us based on who happens to be sitting with us as we gulp down our meal. But when it came to the attention of some Pharisees—we don't know just exactly *how* it came to their attention, whether they barged into the dining room or saw the dinner guests entering the house or heard about it after it started—that Jesus was dining in the company of tax collectors and other people who were commonly thought of as sinners, they thought it was a scandal. Even more scandalous still, it was likely that Jesus had invited them, for the dinner was probably in Jesus' own house or the house where he was staying. At least one modern translation makes explicit what a lot of people have long assumed—that the dinner was at the house of Matthew—but the original Greek doesn't specify *whose* house it was, and the rules of Greek grammar actually support the inference that it was *Jesus'* house and therefore *Jesus'* dinner party. At any rate, it was

Matthew whom Jesus had just called from his tax booth and told him to follow, so it seems more likely that Matthew accompanied *Jesus* to dinner than the other way around. If we have trouble with that picture, as some translators apparently did, perhaps it is because we, too, consider it something of a scandal that Jesus should have sought out and befriended sinners and even eaten at the same table with them without first assuring himself that they had repented—changed their ways. But of course, they *had* changed their ways—had literally changed their direction—when they made the choice physically to get up and to follow Jesus to the place where he was going.

Getting up and accompanying Jesus was the first step for every disciple. Leaving the place of comfort and familiarity and security and ease and stepping into what was potentially turbulent and strange and dangerous and difficult had been a requirement ever since the day that God called *Abram* to believe and bear the promise. And far from insisting that his mealtime companions show their worthiness before Jesus would eat with them, Jesus explained to those who criticized his choice of dinner guests in these words: "Those who are *well* have no *need* of a *physician*, but those who are *sick*" (Matt 9:12). And then he added a quotation from the prophet Hosea: "I desire mercy, not sacrifice" (9:13b). It wasn't their good deeds, even their moral squeaky-cleanness, that qualified them for wholeness, for salvation, but their desperate need, their very sinfulness that left them without any righteousness of their own. "Go and learn what this means," Jesus told his critics. "For I have come to call not the righteous but sinners" (9:13a, c).

A couple of generations ago, commentaries on this passage typically started out with a reasonable explanation for *why* Matthew the tax collector had immediately gotten up from his tax booth at Jesus' command. They usually conjectured that Jesus had surely been evangelizing Matthew over a period of days or weeks or months before this incident, and so Matthew had had plenty of time to think over his choice between collecting taxes and following Jesus, and Jesus of course knew what Matthew's choice would be. But the Bible doesn't give us the slightest bit of evidence of a prior relationship between Matthew and Jesus. The whole point the Gospel is making here is the authority of Jesus to call people to himself—it's not *our* choice to become a disciple, and it's not up to *our* judgment who may *be* a disciple. The Gospels show that Jesus had trouble with those who offered themselves as his followers without being called. They judged their *own* qualifications to follow Jesus, and found their lives to be in proper order, reckoned their devotional habits to be beyond reproach, perhaps regarded their financial situation to be adequate. In their own eyes, their perfection made them perfectly prepared. But as long as they trusted in their *own* perfection, as long as they looked to their *own* abilities—and clearly, they did—they of course had no real need for Jesus; they didn't think that they had any *disease* for this physician of souls to *heal*. Their own calculation of their *suitability* to follow and dine with Jesus *disqualified* them from being called as his disciples and eating at his table.

There has always been a strong tendency in the church, and there is probably some tendency in almost every Christian, by their attitudes and their actions, to turn the *Pharisees* into the real heroes of the gospel—at least to contradict in *practice* what we profess in *words* about the gracious forgiveness of Jesus Christ saving even wretches like us, so that those whom we judge to be sinners, we do not quite welcome to Jesus' table. From the unofficial but effective ostracism that characterizes many local congregations to heated and consuming debates that cripple whole denominations, there is plenty of evidence that the grace of Jesus Christ still creates scandal. In giving *in* to their inclination to judge some people to be *unworthy* of sitting at Christ's table—in judging *some* people to be *too sinful* to be in the congregation or to exercise any responsibilities in it—church folk often set themselves over against the mission of Jesus, and take upon themselves the role of editing Jesus' guest list.

Yet Paul the apostle, often quoted (or *mis*quoted) in support of excluding some from the table because of their sin, their failure to live according to the law, said pointedly, "If it is the adherents of the *law* who are to be the heirs [to the covenant promise given by God], *faith* is *null* and the *promise* is *void*" (Rom 4:13). Look at Abraham, who lived long before the law was even given, and on more than one occasion showed himself to be less than a model of virtue. And yet he was reckoned as righteous. Abraham was not righteous because he was free from sin, but because he responded to God in faith—dropped what he was doing, like Matthew the tax collector did many centuries later, and obediently followed where he was led. In the case of Abraham, he ended up in a new land far from kith and kin. In the case of Matthew, *he* ended up at a rehearsal for the heavenly banquet.

How many good people were sorely offended by Jesus' eating habits, we don't know. How many fathers chose *not* to turn to him in their moment of grief for a dead child? One, at least, refused to let rumors about Jesus' reclining at the dinner table with sinners keep him from pleading for Jesus to raise his daughter from the deathbed, and so she was restored to life. How many women with long affliction decided that they would not, even in their own uncleanness, approach a man who ate with people whom the *law* declared to be unclean? One, at least, refused to let Jesus' unpopularity with the Pharisees prevent her from reaching out behind him in faith to touch the tassel on his robe, and he told her to have courage to face life, for her faith had healed her. The same Jesus who welcomed the unclean to *his* dinner table—the tax collectors and others considered *sinful* by that society—did not refuse, either, to associate with a woman considered unclean because of her menstrual flow or to touch a corpse, also considered unclean, and so give life back to a girl who had been dead. And neither does Jesus refuse to associate with you and me in our uncleanness (and we *are* unclean by biblical standards—just as unclean as any *other* sinner that you can think of). Thank God that Jesus welcomes as his companions people who are sinners! Else you and I would never have any hope of tasting the bread of life and drinking the cup of salvation.

There are, of course, some Christian groups where people are not welcome or are regarded as unqualified if they are divorced, if they speak the wrong language, if their skin is the wrong color, if they are of a particular political party, if they are gay, if they are poor, if they are homeless. That is hard to square with the gracious invitation of Jesus to the despised and outcast of his day to come and dine with him, to be his companions, to have a role in the kingdom, to be allowed into the presence of the Great Physician so that he can *administer* his healing touch and *work* his miraculous wholeness. It is difficult to square with the Holy Spirit's instruction to Peter the apostle that God considers no person to be unclean. Jesus did not rebuke Matthew for making his living by cozying up to the Romans and abusing the Galileans. He asked him to come with him and invited him to be his dinner guest. Jesus did not condemn the unclean woman for daring to sully his sacred tassel. He gave her courage and commended her faith. Jesus did not reproach the desperate father for suggesting that he minister to a corpse. He made *himself* unclean by touching the dead girl and bringing her back to life.

In one of his sermons that he preached when I was in college at Northwestern University, Elam Davies, a Welshman who was for many years the pastor of Fourth Presbyterian Church in Chicago, told of a holiday trip that he and his wife had taken once down to Land's End—that southwesternmost part of England, where the Cornish coast juts out into the Atlantic Ocean. It was just about sunset when they arrived at the famous point of land. It was a glorious evening. The sky first turned brilliant gold, and then bright pink, and then blazing red as they looked out over the water toward the western horizon. By and by, they noticed that they were not alone at that viewing point, but there were an old man and an old woman standing there, and between them, propped up in a wheelchair, a younger man, middle-aged, scrawny, paralyzed, as it seemed, his head drooped forward and his chin nearly resting on his chest, saliva drooling down onto his shirt. How long the aged father and mother had cared for their paralyzed son, Dr. Davies could only guess. But as the sun slipped below the horizon, the father gently nudged the grown boy's chin upward so that his eyes could behold the beautiful picture that God was painting in the sky. "Look!" the father encouraged his beloved child, tenderly propping up his head. "Look! See the light! See the beautiful light!"

A long time ago, our Lord was sitting at table with people who had every sort of spiritual ailment, people he very likely had invited, saying, "Come, follow me." And his very invitation to them was a gracious taking them by the chin and gently tilting their face to where they could see the Son. "Look!" he said to them, and he still says to everyone whom he invites today, carelessly unheeding of scandal but passionately interested only in their need. "Look! See the light! See the beautiful light!" Friends, that is the meaning of grace.

Eleventh Sunday in Ordinary Time
Spanish Springs Presbyterian Church, Sparks, Nevada
June 15, 2008

Genesis 18:1–15; 21:1–7
Romans 5:1–8
Matthew 9:35 —10:8

"Absurd Faith"

A FEW MONTHS AGO, I was having a conversation with a stockbroker who is a member of one of the Presbyterian churches in the area. I mentioned that I had recently asked my *own* stockbroker, after selling a particular stock that I had owned for many years, to put the money into a socially responsible mutual fund. I wanted my money invested in a fund that included neither alcohol nor tobacco, did not support sweatshop conditions or child exploitation, was environmentally sensitive, did not involve the manufacture or sale of weapons, and did not include private prisons. "You're not going to get a very good return," my stockbroker had said, but I told him that, as a Christian, the financial return on my investments could not be as important to me as being certain that I was not supporting or profiting from businesses that are contrary to my faith principles. While it didn't particularly surprise me that my *own* stockbroker questioned such an investment philosophy, it surprised me a great deal that the Presbyterian stockbroker to whom I told the story *likewise* raised *his* eyebrows. "Don't you want the greatest profit?" he asked. "That's how I look out for *my* clients. That's what investment is *about*." I would agree that, in our culture, that is what investment has *become*. Had this person been my own parishioner, I would have continued the conversation, inquiring how any Christian could be more concerned with making *money* than making a *witness*. Under the circumstances, though, at that point, I decided it was better to change the subject.

No doubt, had I asked the man whether he preferred sobriety to addiction, or health to lung and heart disease, or good wages to poverty, or a clean environment to pollution, or peace to war, or profiting from human success rather than profiting from human failure, he would have answered, "Yes, of course." No doubt, had I asked the man whether he had faith in the promises of God and believed that we should live as if God's promises were certain of fulfillment, he would *likewise* have said, "Yes, of course." But had I asked him whether he should align his finances in such a way that reflected his *beliefs* rather than wagering that God's promises are *untrue*, I suspect he would have been at least *confused*, maybe even *hostile*. It must seem absurd to many people to entertain the notion of living as if the kingdom of God were really nigh—as Jesus insisted it is.

Survey after survey discloses that modern Americans have a general, modestly pious belief in the existence of God. To trust that God's power and grace can have a direct impact on contemporary life, working amazing transformations and delivering bounteous blessings, is quite another matter for most people. Where we place our trust shows itself most honestly *not* in *surveys* about religion, but in the way we spend our money, or save it, or invest it. It reveals itself, too, in what we hope for, and the degree to which we are willing to invest ourselves, our time and our effort, to nurture our hope to fruition. Are the things that God has promised in scripture the things for which we invest, spend, live? Or do we regard them really as nothing but *ideals*, nice thoughts too absurd really to put our faith in?

When God promised Abraham (then "Abram") that he would make of him a great nation, it seems that God did not go into any specific details, but it was understood that that meant progeny, descendants. And *that* meant that the fulfillment of the promise would have to start with Abraham and Sarah having a child. Long years went by, though, and Abraham and Sarah remained childless. Out of desperation, they decided to think outside the box, so to speak, and, at Sarah's urging, Abraham fathered a child by Sarah's slave-girl. But Ishmael was not the offspring God had intended, was not the child who would fulfill the promise God had made to Abraham long before. So God reiterated the promise, and made it more explicit. "God said to Abraham, 'As for Sarah your wife . . . I will bless her, and moreover I will give you a son by her'" (Gen 17:15–16a). At that time, Abraham was ninety-nine years old, and Sarah only ten years younger. "Abraham fell on his face and laughed, and said to himself, 'Can a child be born to a man who is a hundred years old? Can Sarah, who is ninety years old, bear a son?'" (17:17).

Surely such a thing was too absurd. Surely God had missed the window of opportunity. Surely the promises of God were not meant to be taken seriously. Surely it was pointless anymore to hope—to invest, to spend, to live as if what God *said* was really *true*. But then, one day in the middle of the day, when the sun was the highest and people customarily took their rest out of the heat, Abraham looked up from where he was sitting in front of his tent and saw three men standing nearby. Quickly, the old man sprang into action to provide hospitality, the principal virtue of Middle Eastern morality. He invited them to rest and permit him to wash their feet—not a minor gesture in a land of little water—and to accept a meal from him—a meal which ended up being much more elaborate than the "little bread" that he first suggested to them. And as he watched them consuming the dinner he had spread before them, they asked him, "Where is your wife Sarah?" (18:9) Abraham nodded or pointed toward the tent. "I will surely return to you in due season," one of the men said to Abraham, "and your wife Sarah shall have a son" (18:10). *Now*, it was *Sarah's* turn to laugh, no more than a whispered chuckle but enough to come to the notice of the men. At this point, the Bible identifies *one* of the men, or *all* of them, as "the Lord." "The Lord said to Abraham, 'Why did Sarah laugh and say, "Shall I indeed bear a child, now that I am old?"'" (18:13)—in fact, she *had* laughed. "Is anything too wonderful for the Lord?" (18:14a).

    Generations of Bible readers have clicked their tongues at the disbelieving ninety-year-old Sarah. She should have known. She should have trusted. Nothing is too wonderful for the Lord. But before we congratulate ourselves on being more trusting than Sarah, we should examine our own record of relying on the promises of God that have come down to us in scripture. We may hide our distrust behind fine-sounding words and phrases and virtues, like "prudence," or "family responsibility," or "common sense." But wasn't it *common sense* that a woman years beyond menopause and a man, how shall we say it, past his prime, would be incapable of procreation? Both had scoffed at the absurd idea of pregnancy, perhaps had rather hoped by then that it *wouldn't* happen.

    Thinking that we guarantee the future by mortgaging the present, believing that we are preserving peace by waging war, arguing that low wages today will assure jobs tomorrow—all of those are pearls of a popular wisdom that is directly contrary to the truth that God has declared in scripture. All of those are, in essence, laughing at God's promises. Those of *us* who laugh at God's promises, or behave as if we think God's promises were too absurd to guide our lives and so we make our plans as if the promises were *not* true, are not only demonstrating our *faithlessness*. We are very likely putting *obstacles* in the way of God's *will*. How many times has God's future of a world without war, of a world in which all people have enough to eat and clean water to drink, of a world in which all people praise the living God not insincerely out of compulsion but earnestly out of love—how many times have these things been delayed by people who tell pollsters that they believe in God but actually live as if God cannot be trusted to accomplish what God has promised? How many times have Christians rationalized away the teachings and commandments of Christ by claiming that the world is not yet ready for his way, cannot yet function by his truth, is not yet capable of finding in him its life? And so, we assert, we must still live by the law of the jungle, tooth and claw (in a socially acceptable way, of course, institutionalizing poverty, justifying the maiming of a generation, willing to do as a *group* what few of us would consider acceptable as *individuals*). "But Sarah denied, saying, 'I did not laugh'; for she was afraid. [The Lord] said, 'Oh yes, you *did* laugh'" (18:15).

The good news is that God serves as the source of hope when the way into a future of peace and justice and equity and wholeness seems entirely closed. Despite the indisputable facts of biology, Sarah gave birth to a son, and then Abraham made fun of his and Sarah's own distrust by naming the boy Isaac, which means something like "he laughs" or "she laughs." Is anything too wonderful for the Lord? It's interesting that we hear no words from Abraham in response to Isaac's birth. In the Bible's telling of the story, at that point, he remains silent. Was he wondering how he was going to pay the boy's way through college? Abraham was not a particularly deep thinker—more a person of action. But on this occasion, I suspect, he was thinking a *lot*—pondering the sort of God with whom he had entered into a partnership twenty-five years earlier to sire a nation that would be a blessing to every other nation on the earth. That promise had perhaps become a dim memory in the daily challenges of moving flocks from here to there, of facing the threats of kings and warlords who considered the land into which God had installed Abraham's family *their* land, of settling the inevitable little domestic disputes that arose among relatives and servants. But God had remembered the promise, and remained true to it, despite every barrier, natural, psychological, social, political. "The Lord dealt with Sarah as he had said, and the Lord did for Sarah as he had promised. Sarah conceived and bore Abraham a son in his old age, at the time of which God had spoken to him" (21:1-2).

Jesus, long centuries later, called to himself twelve disciples and gave them authority over unclean spirits, to cast them out, and to cure every disease and every sickness, promised them the ability, by the power of the Holy Spirit, to do such things as *he* had done, and commissioned them, by way of baptism, to make *other* disciples in every corner of the world teaching *them* to do the *same thing*. We are the heirs of that promise, and the promise that the future belongs to God. That means that the present must bend toward that promise, regardless of what we say are *economic* realities, *political* realities, *international* realities, even *biological* realities. And the way we get from the *present* to the *future* that God has *promised* is not by a waving of some heavenly wand and—poof!—everything is *different*. It comes about through the effort of human beings who have faith in God, an *absurd* faith, even, that God is trustworthy and will use such people as instruments for bringing about the great divine purpose in the world, despite all the complications, despite all the difficulties, despite all who would ridicule or deny, human beings like you and me who refuse to surrender God's promises to the human *il*logic of settling disputes by war and excusing poverty as unavoidable and dismissing hunger as inevitable and accepting disease as the will of God.

I've been a pastor long enough to know that some here will object to some of what I have said, may even be angered by it. Our habitual ways of thinking and looking at things are deeply ingrained, have sometimes even been supported from some pulpit. To have faith is one thing, but to trust our children, our economic well-being, our national security, so much to God?—surely such faith is absurd! But the task of the preacher is not to bear witness to human logic, even to the *consensus* of human logic, but to the will and ways of God, even at their most outrageous, and to summon faith, even at its most absurd. "Then one [of the visitors] said, 'I will surely return to you in due season, and your wife Sarah shall have a son.' . . . Now Abraham and Sarah were old, advanced in age; it had ceased to be with Sarah after the manner of women. So Sarah laughed to herself. . . . The Lord said to Abraham, 'Why did Sarah laugh and say, "Shall I indeed bear a child, now that I am old?" Is anything too wonderful for the Lord? At the set time I will return to you, in due season, and Sarah shall have a son'" (18:10–14). "The Lord dealt with Sarah as he had said, and the Lord did for Sarah as he had promised. Sarah conceived and bore Abraham a son in his old age, at the time of which God had spoken to him. Abraham gave the name Isaac to his son whom Sarah bore him" (21:1–3)—a name which means, "He laughed."

Twelfth Sunday in Ordinary Time
Spanish Springs Presbyterian Church, Sparks, Nevada
June 19, 2005

Genesis 21:8–21
Romans 6:1b–11
Matthew 10:24–39

"Chosenness"

It is probably a natural characteristic of human pride that when we hear that we have been selected for some particular distinction, we rather immediately take it as an *approval* of *ourselves* and a *rejection* of our *neighbors*. There is something about our psychological makeup that turns life into a contest, a rivalry, that gives us inordinate pleasure in thinking that some perceptive person has finally recognized us as more worthy of notice, more deserving of prestige, than the people around us. A few months ago, we received an email through the church internet provider that read: "You have been chosen to participate in an invitation only limited time event! Are you currently paying over 3% for your mortgage? STOP! We can help you lower that today!" You will be relieved to know that I at once recognized that the church couldn't possibly have been selected and preapproved to receive home financing, as has been confirmed by the fact that we have received two or three or more identical invitation-only offers every day since, each appearing under the name of a different sender. Clearly, some marketing firm has sold some lender a software package that dials up every email address they can get their hands on to inform the recipients that they have been "chosen." And then they expect human nature, or human vanity, to *respond* to the flattering news.

The Bible talks about various people being chosen, being selected, being singled out, by none other than *God*. In the Old Testament, chosenness is nearly always for a particular *task*, sometimes a task that will take only a brief time to accomplish, sometimes a task that will take a lifetime, sometimes a task that will stretch out over generations. *Saul* was chosen to be *king*, and then when he proved to be unworthy—apparently a surprise and disappointment to God as well as to Samuel the prophet—God told Samuel to choose *another* to be king—David. And to David was promised the kingly throne of Israel, and a dynasty that would forever *occupy* the kingly throne of Israel. God chose the *prophets*, and often told them that they would encounter difficulties and threats—which they did—and in one case informed a prophet that he would *fail* in the task to which God had appointed him, but he was to do it *anyway*—and he did. Long *before* all that, God had chosen *Moses* to lead the Israelites up out of bondage in Egypt and through the parted waters of the Red Sea and across the wilderness of the Sinai to a promised land—and, despite Moses' manifold objections, he did so. And before *Moses*, there was God's choice of *Abraham* and *Sarah* to be the father and mother of a whole *nation* that God would bless with the gift of the land of Canaan, and which was commissioned to be a blessing to *all* peoples.

In those cases, a close reading of the scriptures reveals that being chosen had at least as much to do with obligation as it did with reward—of being people who were chosen as much to suffer as to exult. In the *New Testament*, Paul speaks of *our* having been selected, chosen, for *salvation.* But our Gospel reading this morning reminds us that that chosenness, involving as it does our being disciples of Jesus Christ, puts us on the path to a very possible martyrdom, bearing the cross as Jesus did, and perhaps quite literally, for "a disciple is not above the teacher, nor a slave above the master; it is enough for the disciple to be like the teacher, and the slave like the master. If they have called the master of the house Beelzebul, how much more will they malign those of his household!" (Matt 10:24–25)—his followers. For what privilege has he *chosen* us, this Savior who has "come to set a man against his father, and a daughter against her mother, and a daughter-in-law against her mother-in-law," so that "one's foes will be members of one's own household" (10:35–36)? There may indeed be a reward for faithful discipleship in *heaven*, but in the meantime, "those who *find* their life will *lose* it"—a prediction that may keep many people from ever embracing that other prediction—"and those who *lose* their life for [Jesus'] sake will *find* it" (10:39). In the New Testament as well as the Old, chosenness really has to do with obedience and humility and servanthood and trust.

There is a lot of triumphalism among some Christians today, a conviction that their discovery of Christ has made them better than other people—despite Christ's own explicit teaching that *his* followers are to consider everyone else as better than *they* are. Many Christians expect personal privilege in *this* world as *well* as the next, including some God-given right to impose their beliefs on others. But such a view of Christian faith is far from biblical, and such a view of discipleship is far from true, either by the standards of Christ's teaching or actual experience. The purest motive for Christian discipleship is not eagerness for what we may get, but gratitude for what we have already been given—newness of life, forgiven and free, through the death and resurrection of Christ Jesus, in whom we have *died* and *with* whom *we too* shall be *raised*.

The entire subject of chosenness or selection by God is so susceptible to misunderstanding that we need to be very careful in the presuppositions that we bring to the faith and to our reading of the Bible. Madison Avenue has done much to increase our sense of being entitled to special privilege, much to inculcate a sense of superiority over our neighbors. So it is scarcely surprising we should *recoil* from the notion that being chosen by the Creator of the universe or by his own Son is actually a promise of suffering and a near guarantee of poverty and rejection and scorn and maybe even death. Since long before the invention of modern advertising, though, racial and ethnic and class prejudice have provided people with excuses for drawing distinctions between ourselves and others who don't look or sound or behave like we do, and to suppose that *we* are the *normal* ones quite naturally favored by God, and *they* are the *aberrations* whose salvation is theoretical at best and even *then* only by some charitable exception. (Hence, a neighbor of mine in another city once commented, in complimenting the landscaping at the house of another neighbor, "Yeah, he keeps his yard real nice for a Black.") And so we may read such passages as the story of Hagar and Ishmael as being interesting but not particularly relevant to us, when in fact it contains a profound message for *anyone* who thinks God has shown insightful judgment in choosing *us* and *not* choosing someone *else*.

Despairing that God was ever going to deliver on the divine promise to give Abraham and Sarah a child, Sarah had offered Abraham her slave-woman Hagar for a one-night stand. Hagar conceived, according to Sarah's plan. But Sarah became jealous when she thought she detected a smirk in Hagar's expression, and, with Abraham's approval, Sarah abused her, and the slave-woman ran away into the wilderness. An angel of God found her there, by a spring of water, and said to Hagar, "Now you have conceived and shall bear a son; you shall call him Ishmael, for the LORD has given heed to your affliction" (Gen 16:11)—rather like God heard and gave heed to the affliction of the Hebrew slaves in Egypt, and then brought them up from their slavery. "[Your son] shall be a wild ass of a man," the angel said to Hagar, "with his hand against everyone, and everyone's hand against him; and he shall live at odds with all his kin" (16:12). And Hagar returned to Abraham's camp, and eventually gave birth to Ishmael.

Abraham naturally had affection for his son, but God appeared to him and reiterated that Sarah herself would become pregnant. "And Abraham said to God, 'O that Ishmael might live in your sight!' God said, 'No, but your wife Sarah shall bear you a son, and you shall name him Isaac. I will establish my covenant with him as an everlasting covenant for his offspring after him. As for Ishmael, I have heard you; I will bless him and make him fruitful and exceedingly numerous; he shall be the father of twelve princes, and I will make him a great nation. But *my covenant* I will establish with Isaac'" (17:18–21a).

After Isaac was born, and Abraham circumcised him on the eighth day, the boy grew and was weaned, probably at about age three, according to custom (Sarah was probably ready), and a great feast was held to celebrate the occasion. But when Sarah saw the older boy Ishmael, the son of her slave Hagar, playing with her own child Isaac, she told Abraham to drive Hagar and Ishmael away so that Isaac would not have to divide his father's estate. Abraham was distressed at the thought of sending his son Ishmael away, but God told him to do as Sarah had said, because it was through *Isaac* that Abraham's covenant-fulfilling progeny would come. "As for the son of the slave woman," God told him, "I will make a nation of him also, because he is your offspring" (21:13). So Abraham sent Hagar and Ishmael away into the wilderness where they feared they would die of thirst, but God appeared to them and showed them where there was water—rather like God would one day give the Israelites water in the desert wilderness of Sinai. And Genesis testifies: "God was with the boy, and he grew up" (21:20a).

That well became a sacred spot for the Ishmaelites—the place where God miraculously gave refreshing and life-sustaining water to the disinherited outcast, the place where God guaranteed that *this* boy, *too*, would *live*, and that a nation would spring from *him*, *too*, and would walk the earth that God created to be a delight, would be *another* family of humankind that God would care and provide for. As God saved the descendants of Abraham's son *Isaac* thirsting in the desert with a miraculous gift of water, so God saved Abraham's son *Ishmael* thirsting in the desert with a miraculous gift of water. The fact that God *chooses some* does not mean that God *rejects others*. The fact that God determined to raise up the nation Israel for a particular purpose, a special witness, does not mean that God's care and concern stops at Israel's borders. The fact that God blessed Abraham and Sarah with the promise of a multitude of descendants and a land of their own does not mean that *other* people are unworthy of being blessed by God; in fact, the very reason God chose one people to be specially blessed was so that they would be a blessing to *others*. God was going to care for Hagar and Ishmael her son, too. But *their* destiny lay in a *different* direction, out in the desert, where they were sent to live like the Bedouins do today, the people who trace their ancestry back to Ishmael and their religious faith back to Abraham. And whatever it means for us in the Christian church to profess that Jesus Christ is the way and the truth and the life, whatever it means that Jesus said, "Everyone therefore who acknowledges me before others, I also will acknowledge before my Father in heaven; but whoever denies me before others, I also will deny before my Father in heaven" (Matt 10:32–33), it *does not* mean, it *cannot* mean, that God's horizon of blessing stops at the *church door*, that God's *love* is *exclusive* to *us*, that God's *purpose* is *limited* to *us*, that God's *salvation* is *intended only* for *us*.

To be chosen by God is a great privilege, but it is not a matter of personal prestige. To be chosen by God is to be given a task, a duty, an obligation, that may make one's life much more difficult, much more demanding, much more hazardous, much more problematic than the lives of other people around us. To be chosen by God is not a recognition of special competence or even a reward for exceptional morality, as far as the *Bible* is concerned. To be chosen by God is to be an instrument of God for the sake of redeeming the whole creation that God loves. So, by definition, as well as by the Bible's own witness, for you or me to be chosen by God does not mean that God is rejecting or excluding *others*, and we mustn't try to regulate God's behavior according to our human preferences. To be chosen by God is a blessing—it is *always* a blessing to serve our Creator—but *no* blessing has ever been intended to stop with the first person who receives it. Our faith in the God who created everything that is with a word has to be big enough to accommodate our humble acknowledgment of and thanksgiving for the *mystery* of God's salvation—the mystery that incorporates you and me in the working out of God's purpose through no merit or competence of our own, the mystery that provides for an *Ishmael* as well as an *Isaac*, the mystery that means that even the least talented, the least remarkable, the least deserving among us may be someone who has been chosen by God.

Thirteenth Sunday in Ordinary Time
First Presbyterian Church, Ponca City, Oklahoma
June 29, 2014

Genesis 22:1–14
Romans 6:12–23
Matthew 10:40–42

"What Sort of a God . . . ?"

A few weeks ago, our new church officers whom we are ordaining and installing today took part in training for their service on the Session and on the Board of Deacons. Among other things, they spent some time examining the various documents—creeds, catechisms, declarations—that together constitute our Presbyterian *Book of Confessions*. All of these documents, though written at different times in different places, though prompted by different circumstances and addressed to different constituencies, have some common features, and make a common witness. And, naturally, they all, or nearly all, begin with a statement about God. We Presbyterians hold these statements to be true in their essential tenets. Those of us who have been ordained, whether as ministers, or as elders or deacons, have pledged ourselves to be guided by their authority. Their words, in many cases, relate doctrines that we can't imagine *anyone* could contest.

So, for instance, the Scots Confession, the great Reformation-era declaration of John Knox and the other leaders of church reform in sixteenth-century Scotland, begins with the words, "We confess and acknowledge one God alone, to whom alone we must cleave, whom alone we must serve, whom only we must worship, and in whom alone we put our trust."[1] Who among us could possibly deny the truth of that sentence? Who among us would ascribe one iota less to God, would suggest any lesser degree of

---
1. *Book of Confessions* 3.01.

obedience, would offer any lesser measure of devotion, would advocate any lesser standard of confidence in God's wisdom and power and reliability? Our basic notions of piety all require professing our faith in God with absolutes and superlatives. God is all-powerful. God is all-wise. God is all-good. Anything less in a seminarian's statement of faith on the floor of presbytery would invite critical scrutiny and very likely jeopardize his or her ordination. And so, in the words of the Scots Confession, "We confess and acknowledge one God alone, to whom alone we must cleave, whom alone we must serve, whom only we must worship, and in whom alone we put our trust."

But then we come to cases. And, in practice, some of the evidence of our lives frankly seems rather ambiguous on the subject. The world that God created has a lot of dangers and inequalities in it, both from nature and from the human heart—many of the *wicked* live in carefree luxury, and many of the *pious* barely eke out an existence; floods and famines strike *believers*, and *unbelievers* get the benefits of gentle rains and bumper crops. Kings, prime ministers, presidents, and governors come into authority with their hands on the Bible, and then betray our trust and squander their mandate. And, harshest of all, people die, sometimes in the prime of life, even in youth and infancy—the children for whom we have made such sacrifice and upon whom we have poured much love and on whom we have pinned much hope. And even the most devout believers, if they are at all honest with their feelings, cannot avoid the question, "What sort of a God is this who doesn't reward the good or at least doesn't penalize the wicked in *this* life in *this* world upon which the Bible seems to say God places a lot of importance? What sort of a God sends rain (and drought) upon *both* the just and the unjust? What sort of a God doesn't intervene to spare the life of our loved one, even the one who bears our name and carries the promise that love endures, that life is good, that God has a purpose?"

Of the various stories in scripture that raise the question, for me, of just what sort of a god God *is*, our Old Testament reading this morning is one of the two most disconcerting. After long years of disappointment, Abraham and Sarah at last had a child—a son, as God in fact had promised. Relying upon God's promise, Abraham and Sarah had abandoned their security— their home in a place that had supported their sheep and sustained their crops and where they had been virtually all their long lives—and, in faith, set out on a journey to a land about which they knew absolutely nothing. And when they got there, they learned that it was to their *descendants* that the land would be given. But *what* descendants? They were childless. But then the miracle had happened. Sarah became pregnant. God, they decided, surely knew what he was talking about. Against every biological statistic, in the face of all human logic, Isaac was born to Abraham and Sarah. And it seemed that, indeed, God's promise was clearly on the way to fulfillment. A new generation had come into being—the first of the progeny that would eventually become a great nation, innumerable as the stars in the sky and as countless as the grains of sand on the beach. They marveled. They delighted. They gave thanks to God.

And then came another word from God: "Abraham! . . . Take your son, your only son Isaac, whom you love, and go to the land of Moriah, and offer him there as a burnt offering on one of the mountains that I shall show you" (Gen 22:1–2). Surely no publisher would accept a manuscript that ignored a father's anxiety at hearing such a command, or that glossed over the discussion between the boy's father and the boy's mother that night, or that evaded the father shouting out in loud objection to what God had commanded. But the author of Genesis goes into none of that. He just says, "So Abraham rose early in the morning, saddled his donkey, and took two of his young men with him, and his son Isaac" (22:3a). He just says, "*So?*" And "he cut the wood for the burnt offering, and set out and went to the place in the distance that God had shown him" (22:3b).

If we were reading this as a novel, or a newspaper article, we would be moved to blurt out, "What sort of a father . . . ?" But it's *not* a novel or a newspaper that we're reading. It's the *Bible*. And so, despite all of our fine confessions and creeds and catechisms, all of our properly-worded statements of faith delivered on the floor of presbytery and our nodding piety in worship and Sunday school, surely we are moved, in our heart of hearts, to blurt out, "What sort of a *God* . . . ? What sort of a God commands the sacrifice of a child? What sort of a God dashes a parent's hopes and dreams? What sort of a God plays a cruel hoax on an anguished heart? What sort of a God . . . ?"

Those of us who were around during the days of Civil Defense radio, when the emergency frequencies were even marked on our radio dials "CD," will recall hearing regularly the announcement, "This is only a test." As readers, you and I are told that God was *testing* Abraham's faith and obedience when God commanded Abraham to sacrifice Isaac; the story begins with the words, "After these things God tested Abraham" (22:1a). It isn't clear that what happened *before* this in Genesis was the reason God felt it *necessary* to test Abraham's faith and obedience—the command of God that Abraham sacrifice his son Isaac seems totally unrelated to the stories that immediately precede it. But whatever reason God had for testing Abraham by commanding him to sacrifice his cherished son, the very child that God had promised Abraham and Sarah and upon whom God had indicated not only that the future of *their family* rested, but upon whom the future of *God's own purpose* rested, too, *Abraham* did not know that it was a *test*. Already the story has struck down a lot of people's notions about the omniscience of God—God didn't know how Abraham would respond to the test; otherwise, the test wouldn't have been necessary, and, otherwise, God wouldn't have said to Abraham after *sparing* Isaac's life, "*Now I know* that you fear God, since you have not withheld your son, your only son, from me" (22:12b). But the story *still* leaves us with questions about the fairness of God, the justice of God, the compassion of God, the question how Abraham could ever think that a voice telling him to sacrifice his own son could be the voice of God *at all*. The story *still* leaves us with the question, "What sort of a God . . . ?"

One commentator has suggested that, since child sacrifice was a feature of *Canaanite* religion at the time of Abraham, God needed to know whether Abraham had at least as much religious zeal as the pagans in whose midst he would be living, so that, in fact, he *wouldn't* be tempted to sacrifice his child.[2] Would Abraham remain *faithful* to *God*, doing whatever *God* commanded, which might be just as demanding as what the pagans thought *their* religion required? If *not*, Abraham and his family might well be absorbed into the idolatrous and murderous ways of the world around them. But that explanation simply won't do! It makes God no better than the cruel little idols of wood and stone, using the devil's means to satisfy God's jealousy. Some commentators suggest that Abraham actually *misunderstood* God's command—that God had really been directing Abraham to sacrifice a ram all along.[3] But that makes the story pointless—a tale merely of Abraham's near-fatal but unexplained confusion.

No. The story of Abraham's obedient preparations to sacrifice Isaac, and of his hand being stayed only by God's last-minute command, is a story about the depth of Abraham's faith which *remained* absolute despite anguish, despite baffling incongruity, despite the seeming senselessness of it all. And *God* learned that, in *Abraham*, God indeed had a steadfast partner in the work of creating a people who would be a blessing to all the nations. *Abraham* learned that the promise of *God* is *trustworthy*—God had already overcome human biology and human reason. Now Abraham would trust the promise in spite of human logic and human anguish. God's command was real. Abraham's response was real. God told Abraham to kill his son and offer him up on a flaming altar. Abraham was ready to plunge the knife into his only son when God said, "No. I've learned all that I need to know." And Abraham looked up and saw a ram caught in some bushes. And instead of

---

2. Bowie, "Book of Genesis," 642–43.

3. This explanation seems to be hinted at in the discussion of "seeing" at Fretheim, "Book of Genesis," 495.

an offering of bitterness and grief, Abraham was able to make an offering of thanksgiving and joy, and to name the place, "The LORD will provide" (22:14).

Not only did *God* learn something about *Abraham* that day. *Abraham* learned something about *God*—that God is God, freely sovereign, entitled to command obedience to whatever God chooses, *and* that God is graciously faithful, never contradicting the divine promise and the divine purpose. And what *you* and *I* need to learn from this story is that those two things are always encountered *together*. God's sovereignty and God's grace are never contradictory, and, inextricably bound one with the other, they are the basis of God's faithfulness. God's will that the world keep spinning, and it *does*, makes trustworthy God's promise to *provide* for us. God's ability to *stop* the world from spinning at a *word* makes credible God's pledge to stand *beside* us in every trial. And God's gracious purpose of *life* made *imperative* the *death* of his own *Son*.

Missing from the story is any information about how *Isaac* responded to his own father binding him with rope and laying him on top of a pile of wood on an altar and then pulling out a knife and pointing it at his heart. On Good Friday, there *was* no ram caught in a thicket. The nails went through the hands, the sword went into the side, and in the heat and the jeers and the flies, no voice came over the airwaves declaring, "This was only a test." "My God, my God, why have you forsaken me?" (Matt 27:46) asked a dismayed son bound to wood as a sacrifice for the sins of the world. And the only answer was a crack of thunder. What sort of a God?

This is the other very disconcerting passage of scripture raising that question for me. But here, I think, in fact is the definitive *answer* to the question. What sort of a God? A God for whom salvation is a deadly serious business. A God who will cut no corners in achieving the sovereign will, which happens to be eternal life, something so desperately important that it may cost an *earthly* life, and often *threatens* to. A God whose love for generations yet unborn, even, imposes a heavy obligation of faithfulness upon *this* generation. A God whose *compassion* is not at *our* command any more than his *wrath* is at *our* command. A God whose *generosity* and *mercy* must never be *presumed* upon, but whose generosity and mercy never *fail*, and, so, can be *relied* upon. And so the key to it all is in two sentences that Jesus spoke on the cross, seemingly paradoxical and yet which cannot be separated in fathoming the way God remains both sovereign and faithful—"My God, my God, why have you forsaken me?" (27:46) and "Father, into your hands I commend my spirit" (Luke 23:46)—and in the resurrection that followed.

Life from death. Infinite joy from unbounded despair. Genuine hope from utter hopelessness. The promise of God kept, though our own eyes and ears, our senses and our logic, claim it was impossible. What sort of a God? In the crucifixion of Jesus, God the Father was testing not just Jesus his Son, but *himself*—God's own faithfulness to God's own purpose. God, I believe, was in anguish. It was not a game. It was not a hoax. It was the ultimate proof of an infinite love. In the *resurrection* of Jesus, the test results are made known—the triumph of a powerful mercy that resolves in God's heart the anguish over human faithlessness. And God's will for the future prevails. What sort of a God? Abraham's heirs and spiritual progeny became numerous, a channel of blessing for the world. The resurrection of Jesus has sealed the promise of eternal life, even in the face of certain death. So "we confess and acknowledge one God alone, to whom alone we must cleave, whom alone we must serve, whom only we must worship, and in whom alone we put our trust."[4]

---

4. *Book of Confessions* 3.01.

Fourteenth Sunday in Ordinary Time
Spanish Springs Presbyterian Church, Sparks, Nevada
July 3, 2011

Genesis 24:34–38, 42–49, 58–67
Romans 7:15–25a
Matthew 11:16–19, 25–30

"We Are Not Our Savior"

If anyone wonders what a two-thousand-year-old letter could possibly have to do with our twenty-first-century society, the answer is written in the daily headlines of our culture and of our denomination. For many people in our time, as in generations past, Paul's letter to the church at Rome is a favorite part of the Bible. For many people in our time, as in generations past, including many who love the book, Romans is also one of the most misunderstood parts of the Bible. It is unquestionably Paul's great masterpiece of writing. It is the touchstone for Paul's teaching about the importance of Jesus Christ. It was central to the Reformation and it remains critical for Protestant theology today, as well as for Roman Catholic and Orthodox theologians as well. It is a virtually indispensable key to the doctrine of grace, and it is the first writing to which many believers appeal when they make a case for adhering to the law. Whether it be reports of synagogues vandalized or a General Assembly vote to rescind a *Book of Order* provision that prohibits the ordination of a whole class of individuals, everyone can agree that Romans is relevant.

But then begins the contentious debate about *how* it is relevant. Some use Romans to support their belief that God has left the Jews behind in the theological dust or, worse, abandoned them to hell. Some use Romans to support their position that the rules of the Bible, or at least a select few of them, are nonnegotiable. A phrase lifted here or there from Paul's letter can be used to argue *either* of those claims. But an honest reading of Paul's entire essay, with careful attention to the situation of the Roman church in the middle of the first century, will help us conclude that it justifies neither anti-Semitism nor legalistic rule-keeping. But neither does it justify *neglect* of Christian *evangelism* nor *freedom* from moral *restraint*. And those extremists on all sides who mine Paul's letter for ammunition to criticize their theological opponents not only misunderstand or ignore the very important point Paul was making, but seriously defame the great apostle of grace and righteousness by trying to make of him an ally in their unholy crusades.

It's a profound paradox that Christianity was able to establish such a strong foothold in the capital of the empire that was dedicated to its total destruction, the very seat of power from which eventually flowed the authority to put to death the Son of God and those who believed in him. Exactly who first brought to the city the good news of Jesus Christ, we don't know. But it found approval among some of the many Jews who were living there and among quite a few non-Jews as well. But there were also many Jews in Rome who *opposed* the teaching of the gospel, and the majority of *Gentiles* who knew about Christianity had a range of responses from complete indifference to warm embrace to open hatred—some of them, very likely, at the urging of hostile Jews. Under the circumstances, it was rather natural, if not very charitable, for Christians of Gentile background in Rome to regard *all* Jews with suspicion, including those who had become members of the church.

In the late forties of the first century, the city of Rome was rocked by a series of riots. Some scholars speculate that they resulted from Christian preaching outside the synagogues. At any rate, blame fell upon the Jews. The Emperor Claudius ordered the Jews to be expelled from the city. So the Christian church in Rome was left solely in the hands of Gentiles. The general anti-Jewish mood in the city probably continued to simmer over the next few years until Nero, who succeeded Claudius as emperor and was certainly no friend of the Christians, lifted the order and permitted Jews to return to the city. When they came back into the church, the Jewish Christians found themselves disrespected, excluded from leadership, and vulnerable to gossip, and indeed their entire Old Testament heritage devalued. Perhaps, the Gentile Christians in Rome seem to have begun teaching, Claudius had only confirmed by *earthly* decree what God had already decided by *heavenly* decree—that, with Christ's rejection and execution at their urging, God's covenant with the Jews had been terminated. Good riddance, some preached, and their strict rules with them! *We* now take the place of God's chosen. *We* now are the apple of God's eye.

Paul, of course, was a *Jew*, had been in fact one of those most zealous to uphold every jot and tittle of the Torah, had been one of the most active in trying to stamp out early Christianity and its claims that Jesus was the Messiah, that Galilean rabbi who had been so careless of the law and so indiscreet in his friendships and so blasphemous in his claims and so liberal in preaching forgiveness. But in the days and months and years since he had been confronted by the risen Christ in a blinding flash of light on the road to Damascus, Paul had come to see all of scripture, all of history, through the lens of new vision divinely bestowed. He now knew Christ to be the goal of the law and the axis of history, the capstone of God's perpetual work of salvation to whom every verse of scripture pointed, including every rule. But Christ himself was not the newest and highest *law* that must be obeyed, but the indispensable *person* who is the *essence* of *God* in every respect, and *with* whom every individual and every nation must ultimately find him- or her- or itself in relationship. God chose the Jews and gave them the law, but they were chosen as God's way to reach out to *all* nations, and the law was never to be an end in *itself*. Paul now understood that. And Paul had come to be the champion not only of extending Christ's invitation to the *Gentiles*, but argued passionately that they need not adopt the ways of the *Jews*, including the law of Moses, in order to be accepted into the family of God.

As a Jew, as a Pharisee, Paul had been raised and taught to think that keeping the law was the way to receive God's approval. A lot of us *Christians* have likewise been raised and taught that our salvation is all wrapped up in not violating the *rules*. There are quite a lot of them in the Bible. The very spiral of sin that Adam initiated had all to do with breaking a rule. Jesus demonstrated in his behavior that, on the face of them, some of the Bible's commands can even conflict with each other, like caring for one's neighbor in need but also not laboring on the sabbath. And for all his seeming to *relax* the law in the eyes of many, Jesus also made it more *stringent* in some regards, like his teachings about divorce and his teachings about slander. But nobody at the time thought that the laws of scripture were so many or so contradictory that it was *impossible* to keep them all. Paul wasn't about to throw up his hands, and *didn't*, at the quantity and the detail of the Torah. When Paul became a follower of Christ and turned critical of his own earlier trust in the law and fierce opposition to the gospel, it wasn't because he considered the law to be no longer relevant and certainly not because he considered the law to be too difficult. The problem was that he had, and all of *us* have, a way of claiming our honoring of the *law* as our *salvation*. But the law, Paul finally realized, not only doesn't bring us closer to God. It in fact pushes us away, insofar as we become confident in our own ability to keep it and therefore have no need to trust God's *love*, and have no need to value Christ's sacrifice on the cross. But the plain and simple truth is, as Paul finally discovered when he encountered the living Christ, *we* are not our *savior*.

No matter how loudly and how often we shout that *Jesus* is the Savior of the world, if we put our confidence in our keeping the *rules*, we're really saying that *we* don't need a *savior* at *all*. If we think we are made right before God by refraining from everything that the Bible calls "sin," we are really denying the relevance and effectiveness of the cross. Paul had thought that he obeyed the law perfectly. He believed that the law fully embodied God's will, and he believed that God's will is good, and he genuinely wanted to do God's will, and he was sure that he could do so by following the law. But what he found was that, despite his being a perfect doer of the *law*, *sin* had control of his impulses and his desires—the law even became for him the *vehicle* of sin, or its *rationale*, inasmuch as it led him to oppose *Christ* who seemed so often to disregard the law's prescriptions and proscriptions. But in rejecting Christ, and in persecuting the followers of Christ who *also* seemed so to disregard the law, Paul was actually rejecting the ultimate expression of God's will, the very person and personality of God, God's living Word. "Wretched man that I am!" he cried in anguish, and in doing so he echoed the moral dilemma of all of humankind and all of Israel. "Who will rescue me from this body of death? Thanks be to God through Jesus Christ our Lord!" (Rom 7:24–25a)—that is, as one commentator has rephrased it, "Thanks be to God, [the one who will deliver me] through Jesus the Messiah, our Lord."[1]

It was because he had placed his confidence in the *law* and his ability to *observe* it that Paul had taken part in actually *rejecting* God utterly and completely. He believed that the law was given by God. It was. He believed that the law is holy, just, and good. It is. He believed that people ought to delight in the law. They should. But touting the law above grace, relying on keeping the law to the point that it becomes sin's very base of operations, persuading us in fact that we can manufacture our own salvation based on our own moral perfection, turns it into the machinery of enslavement. It makes *absolute* what is only *penultimate* and denies God the freedom to work *salvation* by the indwelling Spirit of the risen and living *Christ*.

That was the plight of *Israel* under the *law*, including Paul *himself* before his conversion on the road to Damascus. That is the plight of *Christians* who, despite all their words about God's *grace*, finally render judgment upon others and upon themselves on the basis of the *law*. All humanity faces the same issue, whether Jew or Gentile. We all stand in need of deliverance.

---

1. Wright, "Letter to the Romans," 571.

And our deliverance comes not from keeping the law, good and important as it is, though also susceptible to human contrivance and distinction and judgment, but rather through Jesus Christ crucified and risen, who sends the Spirit to rule our inmost selves.

You and I have known many Christians who are functional nonbelievers in the sufficiency of the undeserved grace of God demonstrated on the cross. And I think that, from time to time, that describes each of *us*, *too*, certainly whenever we lob verses of scripture at each other's trenches, certainly whenever we preach that God has abandoned the Jews and others who do not accept Jesus as the Christ, the Messiah of God, God's own Son, the perfect expression of God's redeeming will for creation, and, I think, whenever we make *any* law or commandment the pinnacle of our gospel. How quickly, like Paul had been in *his* days of dogmatic championing of rules and prideful obedience to the law, we miss the entire point of what God has done for us and for all humankind in Jesus Christ. How often, in the very self-trusting effort to impress God, we have in fact declared with our self-righteous attitudes and our proud, and perhaps hateful, words, that we don't really think that *we* need God's Savior at all. In our quickness to judge others, we are really claiming our own ability to save ourselves. Now *that* is *sin*.

Shall we abandon the law and ignore scripture's commands? By no means. But shall we take it always in the context of the whole gospel and as pointing out our very need for the indwelling of the Spirit of the risen Christ within us? Absolutely. And thus we should preach. And thus we should evangelize. And thus we should confess with all people alike our common need for God and our common recognition that not by keeping *a single law* do we guarantee the approval of God, but only by loving God with all our heart and all our soul and all our mind and all our strength, and by loving our neighbor as ourselves, freed to do so only by the love God has shown us in the cross of his Son Jesus Christ.

Fifteenth Sunday in Ordinary Time

Spanish Springs Presbyterian Church, Sparks, Nevada

July 13, 2008

Genesis 25:19–34
Romans 8:1–11
Matthew 13:1–9, 18–23

"The Bible's Brand of Spirituality"

Our first two readings from the lectionary this morning made me curious to look up Webster's definition of the adjective "spiritual." In the *Romans* passage, Paul is insistent in his contrast of "flesh" and "spirit," and yet the story that the *Genesis* passage tells is all about a very "earthly" situation; you can't get much more "fleshly" than talking about pregnancy and wombs and childbirth and hunger. The *first* meaning of "spiritual," according to my venerable copy of *Webster's*: "Of or consisting of spirit; incorporeal." *Second* meaning: "Of the intellectual and higher endowments of the mind; intellectual." *Third* meaning: "Of the moral feelings or states of the soul." *Fourth* meaning: "Of the soul or its affections as influenced by the divine Spirit; pure; holy—opposed to carnal." *Fifth* and *final* meaning: "Of sacred things or the church; sacred; ecclesiastical." *Antonyms* include: "bodily" and "earthly."[1]

Most of us, when asked, would immediately respond that the Bible is a "spiritual" book about "spiritual" concerns. Indeed, most of us treat the Bible differently from other books, reverentially and with greater deference, even though the very word "Bible" comes from the Greek generic term for any "book." In many of our homes, the Bible will have pride of place on the bookshelf—sometimes it's placed so high in the bookcase that it's obvious it isn't used very much. Some people consider the Bible so special that they

---

1. *Webster's Collegiate Dictionary* (5th ed.), s.v. "spiritual."

are reluctant to *read* it. I recall one man explaining to me that whatever is in the Bible is true, without question. "If it's in *there*," he said, patting the Bible sitting on the desk in front of him, "I *believe* it." Our conversation, though, disclosed that he had actually read only a few very short sections of the Bible, and *that* happened many years earlier in Sunday school. I think that if I would have told him that the Bible says the sun comes up in the west, he would have maintained it must be the *truth* because the Bible *said* so.

A careful reading of the Bible will challenge the popular definitions of the word "spiritual." For the Bible does not discredit the body, nor does it disparage the things of the earth, nor does it discount the concerns of our daily worldly life. Disinterest in the body and the world is a feature of pagan Greek philosophy, not the religion of Abraham and Sarah, Isaac and Rebekah, Jacob and Rachel, and the prophets, and Jesus. Indeed, a good portion of the Old Testament, and even some of the New, reads like a soap opera, so concerned is it with the travails of people who seem not all that holy and the dysfunction of families that seem not all that righteous. Will they ever have children? Will he marry the right woman? Will their relatives ever allow them to have a life of their own? And there is intrigue, duplicity, lying, cheating, jealousy. You name it, the Bible has it—this book that is so popularly revered as spiritual. And it *is* spiritual—the problem isn't with the *Bible*. The *problem* is with our *approach* to it, and the popular misunderstanding of what "spirituality" really is.

In all of literature, there is probably no other plot that is so much an unseemly mixture of biology, history, ethnology, politics, and family dynamics as the story about Esau and Jacob. I've never been associated with a church that has so many sets of twins in it as this one—three families with twins, currently, and previously a fourth. I understand that, of all sibling relationships, that of twins is unique. Neither my wife's family nor mine, so far as I know, ever produced a set of twins, so our firsthand experience is *nil* and even our secondhand experience is *limited*. But I can imagine that the opportunities for rivalry are legion, and the claims for individual attention from the parents are intense. It is impossible, I have discovered, to treat all of one's children exactly equally, but the conscience of a parent must be especially insistent in urging equal treatment in the case of *twins*. Arguments in the playpen, arguments at the dinner table, arguments over inheritance—how spiritual is *that*?

"Isaac prayed to the Lord for his wife, because she was barren; and the Lord granted his prayer, and his wife Rebekah conceived" (Gen 25:21). Here is a prime example of needing to be careful what you pray for. Isaac should have been a little more specific. To give him credit, he had been married twenty years by the time Rebekah conceived—he was already middle-aged when they were married, and now he was sixty, and dealing successfully with *these* two—Esau and Jacob—required a stamina that he no longer had and a wisdom that he never possessed. The kids were fighting even before they were *born*, adding to the *normal* discomforts of pregnancy. "If it is to be this way, why do I live?" (25:22), Rebekah complained. She apparently went to consult an oracle, and received the Lord's explanation: "Two nations are in your womb"—she must have *really* been large—"and two peoples born of you shall be divided; the one shall be stronger than the other, the elder shall serve the younger" (25:23). God wasn't *prescribing* how it *should* be, but was *describing* how it *would* be. Ultimately, Rebekah's own very different treatment of the two boys, motivated by her clear preference for the one over the other, might have greased the skids of family discord and international competition, but apparently the boys' destiny was settled even before their parents started meddling.

"When her time to give birth was at hand, there were twins in her womb. The first came out red, all his body like a hairy mantle; so they named him Esau" (25:24–25). Here, we have a play on words in the Hebrew text—the Hebrew word for "red" sounds much like the nation Edom, and Esau was later said to be the father of the Edomites, as Jacob would be the father of the Israelites. The Hebrew word for "hairy" sounds like Seir, the mountainous region where the Edomites lived. Historically, Israel would be the stronger nation, often at odds with Edom until Israel finally made her a vassal state.

"Afterward his brother came out, with his hand gripping Esau's heel; so he was named Jacob" (25:26a). Here, we have another play on words, but an uncertain one—"Jacob" apparently meant something like either "heel" or "grasp" or "supplant" or even "deceive." At any rate, the connotation was something like "rascal." The implication is that Jacob was trying to keep Esau from being the firstborn, entitled to two-thirds of the father's estate and the right to represent the family in matters legal and religious. That all sets up the story of Esau's willingness, when hungry, to sell his birthright, his entitlements as the firstborn, to Jacob for a bowl of, appropriately enough, "red stuff." "And he ate and drank, and rose and went his way" (25:34). Eventually, Jacob even tricked Esau out of his father's deathbed blessing.

"Isaac loved Esau, because he was fond of game," the Bible informs us; "but Rebekah loved Jacob" (25:28). So neither parent was able to treat the sons equally. Esau seems to have been warmhearted and loving, gentle with Isaac in his old age, generous with his possessions and magnanimous in his forgiveness, unwilling even to hold a grudge against Jacob despite his brother's shabby treatment of him. We may say that Esau lived too much in the moment, too lightly regarded his birthright, including the responsibility of representing his family before God, more concerned for his stomach than his destiny. And yet, based on popular definitions, can we call Jacob any more "spiritual" than his brother, deceptive and cunning as he was, little troubled with notions of "fairness" or "justice," much less what we normally think of as "holiness"? "Those who live according to the flesh set their minds on the things of the flesh," Paul wrote to the Christians at Rome, "but those who live according to the Spirit set their minds on the things of the Spirit" (Rom 8:8). Well, what's so spiritual about Jacob? In fact, what's so spiritual about a book that regards rascal Jacob as a hero, and, derivatively, his scheming mother?

Jacob, at least, was a planner who could think about the future, who could take steps today to help bring about an envisioned outcome tomorrow. "To set the mind on the flesh is death" (8:6a), Paul observed. For Esau to think about his stomach wasn't *bad*; neither the writer of Genesis nor Paul suggests that food is *unnecessary*. But for Esau to have thought of nothing *but* his stomach, to weigh the benefits of being the firstborn against a single meal and find them to be inferior to satisfying his hunger pains for one day, shows a remarkable lack of wisdom. Surely God was justified in choosing the *rascal* as the more worthy bearer of the covenant promise. God did not *forget* Esau, just as God did not forget *Ishmael* in the *previous* generation—each of those two boys, though not favored by the women of the family, grew up to be the father of a great nation, but *not* the nation that had a special obligation to *God*. Jacob had what it would take—even, in next week's reading, the audacity to bargain with God: "*If* God will be with me, and will keep me in this way that I go, and will give me bread to eat and clothing to wear, so that I come again to my father's house in peace, *then* the Lord shall be my God" (Gen 28:20–21). How spiritual is *that*?

The pastor of a neighboring Presbyterian church in north Dallas once shared in our clergy group there that a church member had complained to him that he, the minister, wasn't "spiritual" enough. "What would I look like if I were more 'spiritual'?" he had responded to the man. Actually, *I* had often thought that the minister was a little earthy; his speech was kind of rough, and his concerns tended toward the worldly. But he had managed a complicated physical move of the church from one neighborhood to another, had managed to finance the new building, had secured for that congregation a future that it would not have had in its previous location.

Neither haloed language nor contemplation of heaven's topography identifies anyone in the Bible as God's person. Jacob was, although described as a "quiet man, living in tents" (25:27), a person of action, boldly staking his future on trust in God's promise, daring even to wrestle a blessing out of God in a long all-night struggle. The Edomites—the descendants of

Esau—achieved nationhood earlier than did the Israelites—the descendants of Jacob. The Edomites had a place on the map, so to speak, while the Israelites were not yet on anybody's "most likely to succeed" list. But, culturally, Edom remained stagnant and stationary while Israel passed from being a loose group of nomads to being a society of farmers, and developed a consciousness of being a nation that was in unique relationship with God. Like their father, Jacob, in contrast to his brother, Esau, the Israelites regarded themselves as cleverer, more forward-looking, and more self-controlled than the Edomites. And *God*, the Bible tells us, pinned his hopes on *them*, the offspring of the thinker, the planner, the schemer, Jacob rather than the offspring of Esau, who was willing to give up so much in return for so little.

Ultimately, the *true* hero of the Bible is *God*, not any mere human being. The spirituality of the Bible lies in the testimony it gives to the holiness of God who deigns to love and work with such earthly material as *we* are, not because it ignores or denigrates the humanness of the characters with and through whom God achieves his holy intent. The Bible deserves a special place on the shelf not because it is magical, but because it is truthful, inspiring hope not because it removes *us from* the world, but because it confirms with confidence what *God* is doing *in* the world. And the special place it deserves is where we can easily reach it not to find in its pages instructions for how to *escape* life's trials but to see how God's purpose is being worked out *through* and *despite* them. The Spirit achieves God's will in the most unspiritual of settings, even as the most worldly concerns are being dealt with, even as the most physical sorts of events are occurring. And that is assuring for people who understand that out of the ground we were taken, and to the ground we will return, but that God so values our physical selves that he created, body and soul together, that he raised Jesus from the dead and will raise to new and everlasting life, also, those who set their mind on the Spirit—not some disembodied ascetic rejecter of all things having to do with the senses and history and politics and family and society, but who blessed and sustained the stubborn rascal who believed in God's promise.

Sixteenth Sunday in Ordinary Time
First Presbyterian Church, Dodge City, Kansas
July 18, 1993

Genesis 28:10–19a
Romans 8:12–25
Matthew 13:24–30, 36–43

"Parable of a Patient Farmer"

"The thing I appreciate about the Presbyterian Church," a person once said to me, "is that it takes the teachings of the Bible seriously, but it doesn't condemn people for their failings." Too many churches are in the business of condemning. The fact is, for many people, Christianity is *synonymous* with judgment and condemnation. One longtime member of one of my congregations told me during a visit in her home that she first joined that church because, in *that* church, she was permitted to *dance*! In the congregations of some other denominations in town, she explained, dancing was forbidden as a great sin, as were other amusements. A person indulging in such pastimes could be excluded from church membership or denied church membership in the first place.

Well, dancing seems rather tame in comparison to *some* activities these days. Perhaps, in fact, we ought to consider getting *our* church into the business of hosting dances as a wholesome alternative to the other things that go on after high school football games and the like. I was interested to hear that comment that the Presbyterian Church is not a church which condemns people for their failings, and the observation that too many churches are in the business of condemning. Some denominations, after all, have long distinguished themselves by a tradition of identifying those members who violate certain standards of behavior and isolating them from church fellowship and even family life either by shunning them for a season, or by cutting them off from the kingdom altogether—excommunication—so that the church may remain pure.

What is the proper response for a church seeking to be obedient to the teachings of scripture, when some members seem to be heedless of its teachings? What are the acceptable latitudes of behavior, beyond which deviations cannot be tolerated? The Christian church has had difficulty with this issue for two thousand years, complicated by the human tendency toward judgment that Jesus roundly and so constantly proclaimed to be unfaithful. It is a very difficult thing, isn't it, to resist the temptation to condemn others for what we perceive to be their moral failings? One hears from some people now and then in criticism of a perceived lack of rigor in moral teaching, "Doesn't the church stand for anything anymore?" Always and especially the question is focused upon the moral issues connected with sexual activity, often by folk who seem willing enough that the church ignore the sins of greed and economic abuse, or war-making and oppression, or gossip and defamatory rumor, all of which Jesus addressed in rather direct terms. Whenever it tries to exhibit the *grace* and *sensitivity* that it has *learned* from Jesus Christ, the church finds itself criticized for not showing moral leadership, for being in bondage to the world, for being in league with Satan, and for tolerating impurity in its midst. And there are those who would exclude individuals as a punishment for some sorts of behavior while approving with their silence other activities which the Bible identifies much more unequivocally as sinful.

Surely, there are occasions on which people who have committed blatant immoralities, or who persist in disrupting the peace and unity and purity of the church, should be disciplined. We have as a portion of our Presbyterian constitution a Book of Discipline, which specifies procedures to be followed when someone commits wrongs, as by engaging in wickedness or violating their ordination vows. But even then, the discipline should be applied in a manner designed to restore such men and women to the fellowship of believers in a life of responsible discipleship, rather than as a means of working vengeance or retribution.

Discipline among Christians should clearly speak of love rather than hatred, and should be an anguished last resort rather than the first reaction to wrongdoing. The desire to maintain the *purity* of the church must be balanced by Christ's mandate of maintaining the *unity* of the church and by Christ's call to be *peacemakers*. The "purity" of the Christian church means not only strict adherence to the highest moral standards; the "purity" of the Christian church also includes strict belief in the doctrine of grace and the generous offering of forgiveness and the constant practice of humility. "Purity" can never be spoken of by Christians without the recollection that we, too, are sinners, forgiven only through the undeserved love of God which is meant every bit as much for that *other* person whom we, by our imperfect sight and with our feeble logic, have identified as a noxious weed in God's field. Shame on us, if living by that truth takes the fun out of being a Christian!

Last Sunday, we considered the Parable of the Sower, or more properly, the Parable of the Seed. We saw that the task of a follower of Christ who would proclaim the gospel is to broadcast the good news indiscriminately, without prejudging where it will find root and grow to abundance. Jesus also told another parable about planting seed—this one concerning a man who sowed good seed in his field, but weeds grew up along with the wheat. The weed that is common in grainfields in the Middle East, and what scholars believe Jesus must have had in mind, is darnel, a poisonous plant that resembles rye when it is mature but which, at its earlier stages, is virtually indistinguishable from a blade of wheat. Now when the servants detected weeds in the field along with the wheat, they asked the owner how it was that weeds had grown up among his wheat crop which he had planted so carefully, and whether he wished to have the weeds uprooted. But he replied, "No; for in gathering the weeds you would uproot the wheat along with them. Let both of them grow together until the harvest; and at harvest time I will tell the reapers, Collect the weeds first and bind them in bundles to be burned"—for in that area of few trees, bundles of dried weeds were commonly used for fuel—"but gather the wheat into my barn" (Matt 13:29–30). Whether because it was too difficult to discern which was weed and which was wheat, or because, if uprooted, the deeply-rooted weeds might bring with them the more shallow-rooted wheat, the owner of the field chose to let the grain and the darnel coexist in his field until time for the harvest, when the whole field would be cut, the grain to be preserved to its use and the weeds to be used to feed the fire.

It is likely that the early church felt keenly the problem of what to do with wayward members—people who yielded to temptations to ungodly behavior and attitudes or whose gossip and spite caused division and disturbance in the community of faith. Perhaps even the *original* disciples of Jesus were quick to assess blame and eager to purge their ranks of the disobedient and the lethargic. But the wisdom of the kingdom is often different from the opinion of the world. Like the patient farmer concerned lest any of the wheat be lost by hasty measures, Jesus counseled his own followers and Matthew counseled the church of his day to be sparing in judgment and slow in discipline. Jesus surely recognized the power of the temptation to judgmentalism and self-righteousness, which his *followers* must resist until the close of history. Jesus certainly was aware, too, that the hearts of the outwardly virtuous may hide a much darker wickedness than any that exists in those whom they accuse of wrongdoing. Perhaps Jesus sensed that excessive policing of his followers would cause dissension among the genuinely faithful, so that he was patient even to allow a weed such as Judas Iscariot to remain in his field out of concern for the other eleven blades of good wheat. Is it possible that even in instances of disobedience and disruption, Jesus was vigilant that there be every opportunity for redemption? So it might be that what starts out looking most suspiciously like a *weed* can end up growing into a stalk of *wheat* after all.

The Bible provides many examples of mistaken identity—when God in great divine grace husbanded what *we* would have thought was assuredly a *weed* into an abundantly fruitful stalk of *wheat*. There is no better example of this miracle of changed spots and changed hearts than Jacob, the wily trickster who ended up playing an integral role in God's saving purpose. He had found a way, though born second, to secure the handsome birthright of his older brother, Esau; he had robbed his older brother Esau of his father's blessing; and later he even outwitted the crafty and dishonest Laban, who had cheated him out of seven years' labor. When we read of Jacob in today's passage from Genesis, he is a fugitive. Esau his brother has vowed to kill him, and so he has fled out into the desert where his wits and his wiles are of no use and his fortunes appear bleak indeed. He was not in the least what we might refer to as a "religious" person; he certainly did not anticipate an encounter with God in such a place as where he laid down his head on a rock and fell asleep. But God came to Jacob in a dream, and in those most *unpromising* of circumstances, God made *promises* to be present with Jacob and not to abandon or give up on Jacob and to restore Jacob to his home, and that Jacob's offspring would yet inherit the land and be a blessing to all the peoples of the earth. And, indeed, God was faithful to the promises; all that was promised came true, and Jacob played a most important role in fulfilling God's purpose of salvation. So God overturns human estimations of what is wheat and what is weed. So Jesus instructs us to be patient until the harvest when he himself will make the judgment between what shall be taken into his storehouse and what shall be abandoned. So the church should always refrain from quick condemnation, and must exercise its discipline with much prayer and great humility and generous forbearance.

James Wharton, a Presbyterian minister who was professor of homiletics at Perkins School of Theology, Southern Methodist University, once pointed out in a sermon that, having an Easter perspective on this parable, we can face the close of the age without terror. The eleven remaining disciples had come to know, from personal experience, what a "weed" is. They had also learned what "wheat" is: one who loves God and neighbor no less totally than Jesus loved "weeds" like themselves. There is surely a potential weediness in each one of us, as we have not yet reached the *maturity* to which God is cultivating our spirit. But God's *patience* with *us*, and Jesus' counsel to his *followers* to be patient with *one another*, is because there is just as surely the potential that what appears to be a weed may yet prove to be wheat fit for his storehouse. It is *his* decision to make, not *ours*. So any judgment of "may not," "cannot," "shall not," from the individual Christian to the highest courts of the church, must be made with great caution, and must be understood to be provisional at best. And there is certainly no place for condemnation in the process. For where *we* may see what looks like a weed, the discerning eye of *God* may foresee a harvest of good grain. Matthew presents us here with what might best be titled "The Parable of the Patient Farmer." Isn't that very close to the heart of the good news? Why, it almost makes one want to dance in the aisles of the church!

Seventeenth Sunday in Ordinary Time
First Presbyterian Church, Dodge City, Kansas
July 28, 1996

Genesis 29:15–28
Romans 8:26–39
Matthew 13:31–33, 44–52

"God at Work"

Our Gospel reading this morning is a collection of snapshot-type images which Jesus used to convey truths about the kingdom of God. Jesus was exceptional at using the things of daily life—secular and even earthy objects and experiences—to communicate the meaning of the spiritual. If we let the images speak to us on their own terms, the parables of Jesus express in a sentence or two what whole volumes of theological treatises cannot. So, Matthew included in his Gospel stories observations that a tiny seed becomes a huge bush, that a small bit of yeast raises enough bread dough to feed scores of people, that a plowman would give everything he has to buy a field in which he has discovered a treasure trove and a jeweler would sell his whole stock to possess a perfect pearl, and that a net cast into the sea snares all kinds of fishes, but it is not until the net is hauled in that they are sorted, some to be kept and some to be discarded.

Now, I am not much of a gardener (though I cut and water the grass), and I am not a real estate speculator (I did, however, dig for buried treasure as a child), and I know nothing about fine jewels (although I read John Steinbeck's book *The Pearl* in eighth grade), and I have never had the patience for fishing (I tried it once for ten minutes). But I do know something about how a little starter can leaven a lot of bread dough. Most of you know that my wife bakes sourdough bread—a lot of you have eaten it at home or at church dinners. Some of you are aware that it all started when, just before we moved away from Richmond, Virginia, Sherry McCormick—who, with her husband David, was with our congregation for the retreat weekend two years ago at Scott County Lake—brought a quart jar of the frothy stuff over to our house as a going-away present. During the years I lived in Richmond before my marriage, Sherry had brought me loaves of sourdough bread occasionally, but it was after we inherited the sourdough starter that I picked up several pounds that I didn't use to have. In the middle of a hot and humid Virginia summer, we packed the starter in a cooler and put it deep in the trunk of our Toyota for our move back west, and each night on our journey, we went through quite a procedure to remove the bicycles and the bicycle rack from the back of the car and dig through the suitcases and boxes in the trunk to get the starter out to repack it in ice. The sourdough starter multiplies as you feed it with sugar and potato flakes, so that, if you don't use it each week or so, you have to throw some away or divide it. Whenever we are away from home on vacation, we have to find someone to feed the starter, along with feeding the dog and the fishes. We have given some of it away from time to time (one friend of ours ended up having to drink some of the horrid stuff at an airport to prove to the security guards that it wasn't acid or an explosive), but my wife has faithfully kept it alive, and, most weeks ever since getting it, she has made bread or rolls—well over five hundred batches, it would be by now—and they have all been so good. Over the years, hundreds of people have enjoyed bread which was raised with leaven out of Sherry's single quart jar. Being a minister, of *course* I think to myself every time I look up from my reading or watching the news on television or playing with the children and see her kneading bread dough on the kitchen counter, her hair pinned up, flour on her forehead and her cheeks, pausing now and then to brush a curl away from her eyes, "Ah, isn't this just like the kingdom of heaven?" I'm sure that, at those moments, she is thinking the very same thing.

"He told them another parable. 'The kingdom of heaven is like leaven which a woman took and hid in three measures of flour, till it was all leavened'" (Matt 13:33 RSV). Some newer translations say that the woman "mixed" the leaven in three measures of flour, but this is a case in which the old Revised Standard Version is nearer the meaning; the point, like the parable of the mustard seed, is the seeming insignificance of the beginning—a pale bit of yeast, an unimpressive little seed—and the enormous result—leaven enough to raise about fifty pounds of flour, a shrub as big as a tree. Both are hidden and secretive in their growth—the increase from seed to mature plant cannot be measured day-to-day, and yet the final result is certain; you can't see the leaven at all for the flour, and yet its effect is sure. The farmer simply put the mustard seed in the ground. The baker simply mixed the leaven in the dough. But the miracle of God's nature took over at that point and, without any human coaxing, there came a fruitful result out of all proportion to the original little investment.

The *miraculous* sense of the growth was probably heightened in Jesus' telling about it by the fact that the Old Testament and the rabbis and even Paul usually spoke of leaven as a corrupting ingredient—all leaven even had to be removed from the house at Passover-time, because it was considered "unclean." But Jesus, always free to get people's attention by turning convention on its ear and always willing to explode cozy custom, spoke of the *positive* effects of leaven as being similar to the kingdom of heaven. God is at work, Jesus was assuring his audience, achieving the divine purpose even though human eyes cannot perceive what is happening, even though the kingdom seems as far away as ever or even farther. And even though its influence may seem minuscule at times, God's kingdom permeates the world, and it has a fructifying and stimulating effect that cannot be measured, indeed, may even go unnoticed, by the human senses.

Examples are not far from hand. Think of slavery—a practice perfectly acceptable in the ancient world, which even Paul took for granted, and yet how totally at variance it is with Jesus' preaching and demonstrating the dignity and freedom of every human being. The moral outrage of the world would befall any nation which today moved to legalize slavery, though it was legal in our own nation as recently as five generations ago—a nation founded, we are often reminded, by Christian-minded folk. Even *non*-Christians would object to reestablishing *slavery*, though it was surely the *gospel* which was the leaven for the abolition of slavery not only here, but around the globe. Think of polygamy—nowhere prohibited in the Bible, many of whose great heroes had more than one spouse, still legal in a few places, but even in Muslim Arab countries it is declining in the face of public opinion influenced by the gospel's finer notions of human intimacy and marital loyalty. Our understandings of God's purpose have evolved *beyond* the *literal* word. So, also, think of the growing unacceptability of war as a way to settle disputes—there are still wars, to be sure, but now they are seen as a mark of human failure, not a measure of human virtue—a last resort in the face of overwhelming evil, not the normal way of living, though warfare is a major subject of the Bible and was almost a constant preoccupation of Israel's kings, one way or the other. The testimony of the Prince of Peace has much to do with even *non*-Christian governments recognizing that battle is not glamorous and there is nothing admirable about violence and destruction. (Now, if Hollywood would just come to realize what orphans and widows already know.) Think of the growing recognition among employers that employees' families matter, that fathers as well as mothers should be present in the home and have a hand in raising children, that companies have the moral obligation to promote employee health, both physical and emotional, and the health of their families—maternity leave, paternity leave, family emergency leave, child care in the workplace, flexible work hours, and all the rest. The profit line did not teach that, but fundamentals rooted in God's valuation of the human creature, although smart businesses have always recognized that they never profit by demoralizing their workers. Think of the tremendous resurgence of interest in spirituality in the face of a culture of reckless materialism, of the quest for community in the midst of all that incessantly promotes the cult of radical individualism.

In the face of a large and preoccupied world of hostile governments and fickle crowds, the disciples of Jesus must have felt as if their efforts to preach the good news were not doing much to change the course of human history, perhaps were not even making a lasting impression on *individuals*. Just before this chapter of parables of the kingdom, Matthew tells us that Jesus was being criticized time and again by the guardians of religious custom because of his words and his deeds. At the end of this chapter of parables about the kingdom, Matthew tells us that Jesus was criticized in his own neighborhood and in his home synagogue because of his words and his deeds, and that people took offense at him. Surely, at the time that Matthew wrote his gospel, the *disciples* of the crucified and risen Jesus were experiencing much of the same rejection that Jesus *himself* had faced. So the stories that *Jesus* told about the silent and imperceptible way in which the kingdom grows and spreads to produce a miraculous result, *Matthew re*told to encourage the faithful proclaimers of the gospel in his *own* circle. The kingdom is dynamic, Matthew testified through the parables of Jesus. It is touching every life and every corner of the world in ways that we do not even know, but which will ultimately fulfill God's purpose of redemption. We cannot see the progress according to any human standard, and yet it is certain. We cannot measure the growth by any scientific instrument, and yet it is guaranteed. The gospel is dynamic and contagious, no matter what obstacles are in its way, even if the obstacle is somehow "us." It is like leaven in dough—quiet, but powerful, a yeasty ferment, producing an irresistible change that will deliver the world to a destiny of God's own design.

We Presbyterians are distinguished by our affirmation of the doctrine of predestination—a notion which turns some people away from the Reformed churches. But we Presbyterians cannot help the fact that Paul talked about predestination—it is in our epistle reading this morning—and that Reformed theologians like John Calvin simply picked up on what the early Christian theologians, especially Augustine, wrote about what Paul had said. Actually, what *most* people find objectionable about the doctrine of predestination is not what Paul or Augustine or Calvin wrote, but the ungracious extremes to which others *since* Calvin have *taken* it. "We know that in everything God works for good with those who love him, who are called according to his purpose" (Rom 8:28 RSV), wrote Paul. "If God is for us, who is against us?" (8:31b RSV).

God is at work, Paul testified. What can prevent God from achieving the destiny of salvation and wholeness and restoration and redemption which is God's will? Nothing! Not tribulation, not distress, not persecution, not famine, not nakedness, not peril, not sword, not the seeming indifference to the gospel, not the apparent lack of response to evangelism, not even the world's evident desire to go to hell in a handbasket. Beneath all of the appearances, despite all of the rejections that discourage the faithful and must distress even God, the leaven is fermenting tiny bubbles in the lump of dough, quietly but surely transforming a sinful stubborn world into the kingdom of God, as it is predestined to be. And as we make our way through life, as we try to be faithful to our calling of proclaiming the good news of the gospel and to encourage people to be caring and forgiving and loving and hopeful, we should remember that every street down which Christ sends us has a sign that says, "God at work"—that people the world over are growing disgusted with war, that people everywhere are objecting to inhumane working conditions and insisting that attention be given to employees' health and to their families as well, that human enslavement in all its various forms is being denounced around the globe, that people in every culture are discovering that their lives are quite empty unless they nurture the spirit. The kingdom is not fully here, but it is certain that God's purpose will be achieved. Like the ability of leaven to raise a lump of dough, the yeast of the gospel, quietly but surely, is bringing the predestined result to pass. Have courage. Trust. Go out and minister in faith. For God is at work.

Eighteenth Sunday in Ordinary Time
Spanish Springs Presbyterian Church, Sparks, Nevada
August 1, 1999

Genesis 32:22–31
Romans 9:1–5
Matthew 14:13–21

"Dare to Be Blessed"

People who are expecting a church to give them the one and only answer to each and every question will probably be disappointed in the Presbyterian Church. There are plenty of places you can go today to be told that God has a plan for every moment of your life right down to what brand of corn flakes you will have for breakfast tomorrow, but the Presbyterian Church isn't one of those places. People who are looking for a church that interprets the Bible as a day-by-day account of what happened since the moment of creation and preaches that the Bible gives an hour-by-hour countdown to the end of the world will probably be disappointed in the Presbyterian Church. There are plenty of places you can go today where congregation members are enlisted to do battle against science and are told to prepare for the rapture at the stroke of midnight on December 31 on this date or that, give or take few hours, depending on your time zone, but the Presbyterian Church isn't one of those places. People who want a neat and tidy answer to each of life's problems will probably be disappointed in the Presbyterian Church. There are plenty of places you can go today where honest questions are discouraged and conflicting perspectives are ignored and stubborn doubts are condemned, but the Presbyterian Church isn't one of those places.

It isn't because we don't take the Bible seriously; it is because we refuse to trivialize it. It isn't because we don't take the lordship of Jesus Christ seriously; it is because we realize that scripture is a witness to *faith* rather than an encyclopedia of *rules*. It isn't because we don't believe that history is in God's hands; it is because we believe that God's purpose is the redemption of all creation—a purpose that requires the commitment of *our* hands. So, if anyone wants a spiritual experience that is devoid of mystery and intolerant of ambiguity, the faith tradition of John Calvin and John Knox and Jonathan Edwards and Woodrow Wilson and Pearl S. Buck and Peter Marshall and John Glenn will always fail to satisfy his or her longings. But, as I say, there are plenty of places where Christianity is marketed as a commodity, preached as a set of rules, taught as an alternative to anguished moral struggle.

But if our Christian faith were devoid of mystery and intolerant of ambiguity, what would we do with a passage such as our scripture reading this morning from Genesis? How does our understanding of God and God's relationship with humankind digest the strange tale of the God who is powerful enough to have made everything that is, wrestling all through the night with a mere human being and failing to get the best of him? We cannot dismiss it simply as God acting out a *role* to teach Jacob some lesson or other; scripture offers not the slightest hint that the struggle was any less genuinely exhausting for *God* than it was for *Jacob*. If we are to take scripture seriously, we will have to be honest about what the passage *says* and what it *doesn't* say. We will have to set aside worries that we are somehow blaspheming God by attuning our piety to what the Bible actually tells us.

Jacob, the trickster, the rascal, the one who had bargained for his brother's birthright and stolen his father's blessing and swindled away his father-in-law's property, was on his way to meet his brother. He was obeying God's command to return to his homeland after twenty long years of absence. Jacob had been born grasping his brother Esau's heel; he was the second of twins, and even coming out of the womb, he was striving for advantage. In biblical times, the firstborn male was favored, receiving the majority of the father's inheritance and the prestige of someday becoming head of the family. Jacob had taken advantage of his brother's *hunger* one time, buying his birthright for a bowl of food. Later, he had tricked his blind and dying father Isaac into bestowing upon *him* the blessing that was intended for his *brother*.

Bold and brash as a youth, now Jacob was afraid of his brother Esau's anger over the past wrongs that he had done to him. Jacob had learned that Esau was waiting for him and had four hundred men with him. It sounded a lot more like a war party than a welcoming committee. Ever the schemer, Jacob had thought of appeasing Esau with gifts, hoping to spare his life by giving up all of his possessions, livestock and servants, but could he *buy* a peace that he had done his best to destroy so long ago? He sent the gifts on ahead in two batches, and that night he sent his wives and their servants and his eleven children on ahead as well.

> "O God of my father Abraham and God of my father Isaac, O LORD who said to me, 'Return to your country and to your kindred, and I will do you good' I am not worthy of the least of all the steadfast love and all the faithfulness that you have shown to your servant, for with only my staff I crossed the Jordan. . . . Deliver me, please, from the hand of my brother, from the hand of Esau, for I am afraid of him. . . . Yet you have said, 'I will surely do you good, and make your offspring as the sand of the sea, which cannot be counted because of their number.'" (Gen 32:11–12)

So Jacob spent that night there at the ford of the Jabbok River near where it flows into the Jordan, hoping against hope that his offer of all his possessions would keep Esau from taking his life. And he was alone in the dark with his fears, the gurgling brook the only sound, the starry sky the only light, and overwhelming anxiety his only companion. The cocky and self-confident Jacob was literally at his wit's end. Everything now rested on the faithfulness of the God who had covenanted with Abraham and his descendants to form them a people and multiply their offspring and give them a land and be their God.

Suddenly there fell upon him a man, and they wrestled all through the night. They were evenly matched in the struggle—neither prevailed. Who was he, this mysterious assailant out in the loneliness of the desert? A thief? An angel? Esau, perhaps, twenty years after they had last parted? Apparently, Jacob did not know; it was dark, after all. Eventually, as the day was dawning and sunlight would soon reveal the stranger's face, seeing that he did not prevail against Jacob, "[the man] struck him on the hip socket; and Jacob's hip was put out of joint as he wrestled with him. Then he said, 'Let me go, for the day is breaking.' But Jacob said, 'I will not let you go, unless you bless me.' So he said to him, 'What is your name?' And he said, 'Jacob.' Then the man said, 'You shall no longer be called Jacob, but Israel, for you have striven with God and with humans, and have prevailed'" (32:25b–28). And it became plain to Jacob, if he had not guessed it before, that it was *God* with whom he had struggled all through the night, and that he had *wrestled* God—at least in this mysterious human form—to a draw. And if you think about it, a draw, for the God who created the universe, is a rather humiliating result of an all-night struggle. "You shall no longer be called Jacob," said the assailant, revealing his identity, "but Israel, for you have striven with God and with humans, and have prevailed" (32:28).

Jacob, of course, was injured in the struggle. Some commentators have declared this to be a mark of *humility*—God had put Jacob in his rightful place for having been such a scalawag up until then. But it seems more true to say that Jacob's injury was actually a badge of victory. It wasn't because Jacob's *personality* had *changed* that God gave him a new name. The new name was based on who he was and how he had *always* behaved. Now, he had struggled with God and was alive to tell about it—had seen God's face, even, though not in the full light of day. And, on top of that, he had even gotten a blessing from God after the all-night wrestling match—the eve of what he fully expected to be a day of battle between himself and his brother Esau. "So Jacob called the place Peniel, saying, 'For I have seen God face to face, and yet my life is preserved'" (32:30). This is long before George Lucas sent Luke Skywalker into a cave to battle *his* fears, but there is undoubtedly a psychological dimension to this confrontation that we should acknowledge. If Jacob had been able to hold his own against *God*, what did he have to fear from *Esau*? And the episode ends with Jacob limping down the road toward the promised land as the sun's first rays peek over the horizon.

The word "Islam"—the religion started by Mohammed—means "submission," that is, "submission to God." Sometimes, Christians think that God expects *them* to be unquestioningly submissive to God in all things and at all times. But the *Israelites* understood *their* relationship to God as a *dynamic* one, of give and take, of *struggle* even, sometimes played out in history as struggle with their neighbors, like their ancient struggle with the Edomites, the nation founded by Jacob's brother Esau. It was not a matter of the passive, unquestioning submission of weak, mindless creatures fetching, rolling over, and playing dead for their master-creator. And if we read the Bible carefully, we detect that God doesn't want that from humankind, anyway. God created us to have a *relationship* with us, and that means a *two-way* relationship, nothing less than a *friendship* based on mutuality, dialogue, mutual respect, joint responsibilities, growing up and growing closer through shared experiences. To deny that is, I think, to deny the testimony of scripture. It may be that God does not *need* us in the strictest sense of that word, but God certainly *wants* us, and perhaps *desire* is an even more powerful motivation for action than *necessity* is. Jacob could not escape from God's grasp, but, remarkably, neither could *God* escape from *Jacob's*. They remained entangled all through the night, and the resolution of the struggle was when God gave Jacob a blessing, as he asked for.

Why did God wrestle with Jacob at the River Jabbok? Was it to give Jacob confidence for his meeting with Esau? I don't think so, because I don't see any evidence that God intended to lose the wrestling match. Was it to teach Jacob a lesson that would turn his life around? I don't think so, because the name God finally bestowed upon Jacob *celebrated* his scrappy attitude toward life, didn't *criticize* it, and though Jacob's *body* was *crippled*, his *character* remained *unchanged*. What does it all mean? I suspect that even the writers of Genesis did not know. The story is told in a tone of deep mystery, and I think the Bible respects that mystery, allows it to remain, lets it stand. But they must have believed that Jacob's and God's grappling with each other during Jacob's hour of fear, during his time of danger when the entire promise of God delivered in the covenant with Abraham and renewed with Isaac and Jacob himself seemed to hang in the balance, was important not only in their nation's *history*, but in their nation's *present* and *future*. And as full heirs to the promises God made to Abraham and his descendants, it must have some importance for *us*, too.

Genuine faith in God, honest engagement, heart to heart and mind to mind, cannot happen if we are denied the opportunity to ask questions, or blandly accept answers that do not square with experience, or are made to think that God isn't interested in our opinions as moral beings or doesn't value us as partners in shaping the destiny of creation. And then, perhaps, we deny ourselves the greatest blessings of insight and understanding, true inner peace, friendship and even partnership with God. When have you faced fears, anxieties, long nights when you felt utterly alone and helpless? When have you recognized that the pat answers no longer convince you, that the *easy* explanations do not correspond to the facts and the fears and the feelings? When have you sensed that the world was closing in on you and events seemed about to disprove everything you had always thought you believed about the goodness of God and the promises of God and the faithfulness of God? When did it seem to you that justice was about to be denied and hatred was about to triumph? When did you dread the coming day when you had to encounter your brother or sister whom you had wronged in some way, or from whom you were estranged?

It's a universal experience, when, as the saying goes, the chickens come home to roost. We want compassionate sympathy from *God* because we expect a hostile struggle with our *foe*. *Jacob* got just the *opposite*—God *assaulted* him, and *Esau*, it turns out, *greeted* him with hugs and kisses! Is there, here, some indication that we can never meet our fellow human beings aright until we have encountered God? That we can't be reconciled to our earthly brother or sister until we have contended with our divine parent? That God breaks into lives at the most needful moment, neither to overpower us with supernatural might, on the one hand, nor to extricate us from our predicament, on the other hand, but to be a partner in our wrestling with questions that have no easy answers, dilemmas that have no quick solutions, mysteries that must remain mysteries until the end of time, but encouraging us to trust always and ultimately in the promises of God which, though absolute, involve human choices and require human action and are worked out through the course of human history? (Remember how Jesus told his disciples when they spoke to him about all the hungry people, "*You* give them something to eat" [Matt 14:16b].) Isn't it those who dare to struggle honestly with the God who wants a true relationship with us—those who are bold to ask difficult questions and have such courageous faith that they are able to live with ambiguous answers, those who understand that *they* have a genuine active responsibility for the achievement of God's purpose, those who stand before the vast mystery of God and yield to its wondrous though often painful embrace—aren't *they* the ones who go limping off toward the promised land as the rising sun dispels the fearful gloom of their night? "Then [the one with whom Jacob had wrestled] said, 'You shall no longer be called Jacob, but Israel, for you have striven with God and with humans, and have prevailed.' . . . And there he blessed him" (Gen 32:28–29).

Nineteenth Sunday in Ordinary Time

Spanish Springs Presbyterian Church, Sparks, Nevada

August 10, 2008

Genesis 37:1–4, 12–28
Romans 10:5–15
Matthew 14:22–33

"God's Dream"

What a time of *optimism* the 1960s was. To a youth growing up in that era, it seemed that the balance was finally tipping toward justice, an end of war, an intolerance of poverty, a rejection of racism. What a time of *despair* the 1960s was. To a youth growing up in that era, it seemed that the self-satisfied establishment was stubbornly intransigent, its strident critics were frequently self-indulgent, and the flames of hatred were growing ever more destructive, with increasing body counts on a faraway battlefield, accusations that the poor preferred welfare to work, segregationists vowing that blacks and whites must, should, and would remain separate. Idealism was high, but fragile. The bastions of power seemed impenetrable.

There were some bold and hopeful voices among us that enunciated a vision different from the reality that we were experiencing—dreams—and some of them were murdered in an attempt to put an end to the dreams. Politicians were shot to death. Prophets were shot to death. Protesters were shot to death. Cities were set ablaze. Society itself bled from the wounds caused by all of the carnage abroad and the conflicts and clash of expectations and interests at home. And over the next few decades, the dreamers seemed little by little to disappear, replaced by the din of bald and unapologetic assertions of personal interest. No longer were we lifted up by dreams of a more equitable society, but our sense of community was weakened by wishes of private fortune, and those few who dared to call for a common vision and to summon us to a common sacrifice and to appeal to the common good were ridiculed and marginalized, even by some leaders of communities of faith.

How often, throughout history, has society been unable to tolerate the dreamers! How often, throughout history, has society found some means of silencing the dreamers! How often, throughout history, has society judged the dream to be a nightmare! And yet the Bible is very clear: the will of God is often communicated in dreams; God often uses the dreamers to nudge the world closer to the day of salvation.

Joseph was a dreamer. The son of Jacob by his beloved wife Rachel, Joseph was specially loved by his father, who had the amazingly poor judgment to flaunt his favoritism in various ways. When he had gone to meet Esau his brother, whom he feared, Jacob arranged the family members so that Rachel and Joseph were last in the entourage, farthest from the potential harm that Jacob feared a vengeful Esau might inflict on the brother who had cheated him multiple times. And when the boy Joseph was seventeen, his father made him a dress coat, far finer than anything his brothers had to wear, and they hated him for it—Joseph, that is, not Jacob who had created the problem by his unequal treatment of his children.

Joseph, himself not too wise in such things, announced to his older brothers that he had had a dream that they were all going to bow down to him. If it were to come to pass—and dreams were considered full of divine significance in ancient times—it would constitute a flagrant violation of the rule that the *oldest* son should be primary in inheritance and in authority. The disclosure of such a dream was guaranteed to win the enmity of the other brothers. "His brothers said to him, 'Are you indeed to reign over us? Are you indeed to have dominion over us?' So they hated him even *more* because of his dreams and his words" (Gen 37:8).

And then Joseph had *another* dream, which he was tactless enough to talk about—the sun and moon and eleven stars would bow down to him. Even *Jacob* objected to *this* dream, when he heard about it: "'What kind of dream is this that you have had? Shall we indeed come, I and your mother and your brothers, and bow to the ground before you?' So his brothers were jealous of him, but his father kept the matter in mind" (37:10b–11).

That's how things stood when Jacob decided to send Joseph the favored one, who apparently considered himself exempt from physical labor, to the territory where the other sons had herded the flocks to pasture, and to report back to Jacob what they were doing. "They saw him from a distance, and before he came near to them, they conspired to kill him. They said to one another, 'Here comes this dreamer. Come now, let us kill him and throw him into one of the pits; then we shall say that a wild animal has devoured him, and we shall see what will become of his dreams'" (37:18–20).

Commentators have noticed that this story never refers to God. But those who have been following along in Genesis the route of the covenant that God made with Abraham generations earlier understand that the promise now rested on Joseph's shoulders—*he* was the son for whom Jacob and Rachel had longed and waited. Those who have followed the story know that any attack on *Joseph* was an attack on *God*. The attempt to put an end to the *dreamer* was *really* an assault on *God* who had put the dreams into Joseph's head. Indeed, unbeknownst to Joseph's brothers, it wasn't just *Joseph's* dreams of superiority that they wanted to put an end to; it was *God's* dreams—dreams of forming a people in covenant with him, constituting a blessing upon the whole creation. And, reading on, we learn that God would not let the dreams be invalidated, for they represented the will of God, and were the very word of God, which, once spoken, never fails of its purpose, never returns empty. Try as they might to kill the dream by destroying the dreamer, the dreams came to pass, and the will of God was fulfilled in a most unexpected way. And as a result, not only were the people *Israel* saved from starvation, but the people of *Egypt* as well.

In a prosaic culture where those who have made the economy into its god never want to consider anything but the bottom line, dreamers are regarded as unproductive, distractions from what is real, dangerous to themselves and others. But I suspect that creation itself was born in a dream—"Ah," said God to himself, for there was no other, "that is what I will do, and it will be good, and it will be fine, and justice shall be its rule, and mercy its method, and plenty its promise, and love its essence." Joseph's father, Jacob, had had a dream once, in the desert—a dream of God's everlasting care for Jacob and his descendants. A prophet once offered a forlorn nation a vision of God's outpouring of the spirit upon all flesh, and in that day, he promised, "your sons and your daughters shall prophesy, your old men shall dream dreams, and your young men shall see visions" (Joel 2:28). And one old man, at the dawning of God's new age, had a dream that his young fiancée had conceived by the work of the Holy Spirit and would bear a son who would save the people from their sins; the Lord continued to speak to the man—another Joseph—in dreams, advising him what to do to escape the harm that the powerful authorities wished to do to the boy. Later, it was because of his wife's troubling dream that *Pilate* left the fate of Jesus to the crowd—Pilate who *had* been disposed to set Jesus *free*, but that would have meant no cross, and therefore no salvation.

But *salvation* was necessary to the achievement of *God's* dream. And so, again, in a most unexpected way, God worked his divine will from what surely had all the appearance of an unmitigated disaster—the death of his very own Son. Once again, the powers that valued the way things were, that praised stability above justice and predictability over miracle, thought that they had killed the dream by destroying the dreamer—had put an end to talk of good news for the poor and release for the captives and recovery of sight for the blind and the arrival of the year of the Lord's favor, which sounded a lot like the jubilee call for cancellation of debts and return of ancestral properties and respite from production. They thought they had put an end to the possibility of a kingdom in which those who were humble and of least account would be raised up and those who exercised worldly power and authority to their own benefit would be cast down. They thought they had put an end to the prospect of sinners and foreigners and women and the sick and the outcast having access to the temple and a seat at society's table. And they thought they had put an end to the notion that anyone could have salvation without having *earned* it. But the dream was powerful, not just because of *what* it was, but because of *whose* it was—not just *Jacob's*, not just *Joseph's*, not just the *other* Joseph's, but *God's*.

"I have a dream" is the memorable phrase giving cadence to one of the most famous public pronouncements ever made in our nation. Dr. Martin Luther King Jr., a minister, knew full well the power of dreams, particularly dreams that communicate the stubborn saving will of God.

> I have a dream that one day this nation will rise up and live out the true meaning of its creed: "We hold these truths to be self-evident that all men are created equal."
>
> I have a dream that one day on the red hills of Georgia the sons of former slaves and the sons of former slave owners will be able to sit down together at the table of brotherhood.
>
> I have a dream that one day even the state of Mississippi, a state sweltering with the heat of injustice, sweltering with the heat of oppression, will be transformed into an oasis of freedom and justice.
>
> I have a dream that my four little children will one day live in a nation where they will not be judged by the color of their skin but by the content of their character.
>
> I have a dream today. . . .
>
> I have a dream that one day every valley shall be exalted, and every hill and mountain shall be made low, the rough places will be made plain, and the crooked places will be made straight, and the glory of the Lord shall be revealed and all flesh shall see it together.[1]

---

1. King, "I Have a Dream."

What is the power of dreams that mirror God's dream? What is the power of dreams that are not mere fantasy but are genuinely prophetic? Later this month, for the first time in American history, two and a quarter centuries after the Declaration of Independence and the Bill of Rights, a century and a half after the Emancipation Proclamation, nearly half a century after the March on Washington for Jobs and Freedom, an African American will be named the presidential nominee of a major American political party. What is the power of dreams?

Throughout the Joseph stories, Joseph's many adversaries resisted God's dream, but they all failed. Some thought that Joseph's dreams were the product of Joseph's own arrogance, a selfish and fantastic wish to turn the ways of the world upside down, but actually they were the voice of God, announcing God's future in which the structures of authority will indeed be inverted and the weak will triumph over the strong and the poor will fare better than the rich and the hungry will be satisfied while the well-fed will have to go begging. No wonder, in every age, there have been a lot of people who wanted to silence the dreamer, to put an end to such dangerous thoughts, to nip any such possibilities in the bud! But God has a dream. Violence shall not prevail. Nor vindictiveness. Nor wealth. Nor earthly title. Nor fame. Those whom society regards as expendable will be revealed to be the chosen ones of God. And justice shall reign. And mercy. And peace. Just a dream? Or *God's* dream, which is even now becoming the world's reality?

Twentieth Sunday in Ordinary Time

First Presbyterian Church, Dodge City, Kansas

August 18, 1996

Genesis 45:1–15
Romans 11:1–2a, 29–32
Matthew 15:10–28

"What *God* Intends"

In the movie *Field of Dreams*, based on W. P. Kinsella's book *Shoeless Joe*, one of the baseball players who shows up in that enchanted baseball park in the middle of an Iowa cornfield is a teenage wannabe major leaguer known to baseball historians as "Moonlight" Graham. Ray Kinsella, the farmer who had mowed down his cornstalks and manicured his patch of nostalgia, had picked the boy up hitchhiking along the highway as Ray was driving home to Iowa from Chisholm, Minnesota. Ray had been magically led to Chisholm to find out about a now-dead baseball player who had only gotten to play *one inning* in a major-league game and *never* got to bat. What had it been like to have come so close to being a big-league player, and not to have been able to fulfill the dream? Another piece of magic happened after Ray Kinsella arrived at Chisholm—the clock turned back some sixteen years, and he had an encounter with that very baseball player, then an aged physician, Dr. Archibald Graham. "It was like having it this close to your dreams, and then watching them brush past you," Dr. Graham explained, "like a stranger in a crowd."[1] It was the last game of the 1922 season for the New York Giants, and the team had a comfortable lead in the bottom of the eighth inning. Graham had been sitting on the bench ever since being called up from the minors. With nothing to lose, the manager sent him out to play

---

1. *Field of Dreams*, 1989, directed by Phil Alden Robinson (produced by Gordon Company, released by Universal Pictures).

right field in the top of the ninth, but he never got to make a play, and the game was over before he could get to bat. He couldn't bear the thought of spending another season in the minor leagues, so he quit baseball and went back to college. "You know," he told Ray, "we just don't recognize the most significant moments of our lives when they're happening."[2]

But it was as a lifelong physician, rather than a one-inning ballplayer, that the little town of Chisholm idolized Archibald Graham. He had made quite an impact, delivering an untold number of babies, setting perhaps thousands of broken bones, easing perhaps hundreds of mortals across the threshold of death. "If you could do anything you wanted," Ray suggested, "if you could have a wish—"

"You know," said Doc Graham,

> I never got to bat in the major leagues. I'd have liked to have that chance, just once, to stare down a big league pitcher, to stare him down and just as he goes into his wind-up, wink, make him think you know something he doesn't. That's what I wish for—a chance to squint at a sky so blue that it hurts your eyes just to look at it—to feel the tingle in your arm as you connect with the ball, to run the bases, stretch a double into a triple, and to flop face-first into third, wrap your arms around the bag.

Ray invites Doc Graham to come to Iowa, to that field of dreams, but the old man declines. Ray is amazed. "Fifty years ago, for five minutes, you came this close. I mean, it would kill some men to get that close to their dream and not touch it. They'd consider it a tragedy."

"Son," said the kindly old man, "if I'd only gotten to be a doctor five minutes, now that would have been a tragedy."[3]

The next day, Ray is astonished when the young baseball hopeful climbs into his Volkswagen bus on the side of the road and introduces himself as Archie Graham—Doc Graham, long before he *was* a doctor. But the boy is a good ballplayer, as he shows when they reach Ray's farm, and young Archie Graham is invited to play by the other ballplayers of old who keep emerging from the cornfield and then disappearing into it again. Archie Graham hits a sacrifice fly that scores a run, but he himself never gets to tag a base.

As Ray and his wife and his daughter, Karin, hot dog and soft drink in hand, sit on the bleachers watching the game one afternoon, while the rest of the world thinks they're crazy for building a ballpark and for watching games that no one else can see, little Karin tumbles from the bleachers and

---

2. *Field of Dreams.*
3. *Field of Dreams.*

her body hits the ground with an unconscious thud. Ray and his wife are panicked at the thought that their precious child is badly injured, perhaps dying, as they jump down from their seats and kneel beside her. Play on the ballfield has stopped; young "Moonlight" Graham sees the crisis from where he is standing on the field. Ray looks at him, aware that this young man is the future physician, the man beloved by a town for having given up claim on his own intentions. It is one of the most poignant moments in the film. A human life is in danger; two desperately anxious parents are in need. "Moonlight" Graham drops his glove and walks across the field toward the bleachers.

As he steps off of the magical field, he is no longer the youthful ballplayer "Moonlight," but becomes the kindly old "Doc," medical bag in hand, who bends down and quickly examines the girl. "This child is choking to death," he says, slapping her on the back, and he extracts a piece of unchewed hot dog from her throat. "Hot dog. Stuck in her throat. She'll be all right," he says, reassuringly.

"Thank you, Doc," Ray says.

"No, son, thank *you*."

And Ray now realizes that, having stepped off of the field, it is not possible for "Moonlight" Graham to cross the threshold again, to go back to being the youthful ballplayer. "I'm sorry."

"It's all right," Doc Graham says, turning to leave, and then he pauses to say to the players, "Win one for me sometime."

Just before Doc Graham disappears into the cornfield, Shoeless Joe Jackson calls out to him, "Hey, rookie, you were good."[4]

A group of brothers, jealous and fed up with their father's favoritism toward another of their brothers, Joseph, scheme to kill the boy and be done with his insulting dreams and arrogant behavior. But one of them can't quite bring himself to take part in murder, and, so, he suggests instead that they sell the boy to a caravan that happens to be passing by. The caravan takes him to Egypt, where, through a series of remarkable events, the boy ends up being the Pharaoh's highest-ranking and most trustworthy assistant, by his wisdom and skill anticipating and preparing for a long famine by storing up great quantities of grain during years of abundance, and, so, saving the Egyptian people from starvation. The famine strikes not only Egypt, but also the faraway land where Joseph's father and brothers live, and his brothers eventually come down to Egypt looking for food to take back home. They are shown into the presence of Joseph, who, now grown to adulthood, recognizes *them*, but *they* do not recognize *him*. After several interviews, he

---

4. *Field of Dreams*.

finally discloses his identity to his shocked brothers, now afraid that they are at the mercy of the powerful sibling whom they had treated so ill. But Joseph is merciful and discerning, and offers to provide for them. "I am your brother, Joseph, whom you sold into Egypt. And now do not be distressed, or angry with yourselves, because you sold me here; for God sent me before you to preserve life. . . . God sent me before you to preserve for you a remnant on earth, and to keep alive for you many survivors. So it was not *you* who sent me here, but *God*; and he has made me a father to Pharaoh, and lord of all his house and ruler over all the land of Egypt" (Gen 45:4b-5, 7-8). After Joseph's father and brothers all came to live in Egypt, Joseph's father died, and his brothers feared that Joseph might change his kind behavior and treat them harshly as revenge for their abuse toward him so many years before. "But Joseph said to them, 'Do not be afraid! Am I in the place of God? Even though *you intended* to do *harm* to me, *God* intended it for *good*, in order to preserve a numerous people, as he is doing today'" (50:19-20).

Joseph's life had not turned out as he had expected, though his dreams which everyone interpreted as meaning that he would rule over his brothers had in fact come to pass. But God had worked his saving purpose through Joseph's life. *Field of Dreams* is not so explicitly theological, but people of faith would conclude that, according to the story, God had worked his saving purpose through the life of "Moonlight" Graham. He had had one inning in the big leagues, and had decided to *quit* rather than be sent down again to the minors. Suppose he *had* gotten to bat at that final game of the '22 season, and had an impressive hit? He would not have gone back to school, would never have become a doctor. His life would have been very different; he might have been famous far beyond Chisholm, Minnesota. But, then, the lives of the people of Chisholm, Minnesota, would have been very different, too, and the life of a little girl in Iowa would have ended tragically on a baseball-perfect summer's afternoon. "You can't go back," Ray said to the doctor after his daughter had been revived, just then realizing that "Moonlight" Graham's baseball career had once again been cut short. "I'm sorry."

"It's all right," said the man whose years of medical experience had just saved a little girl's life.

For very few of us does life turn out as we expected. Being a minister in Dodge City, Kansas, is a long way from oceanography, both geographically and otherwise—that's what *I* was planning on when I graduated from high school. It's a long way from practicing law for an international mining company in Vancouver—that's what I was dreaming of when I graduated from college. It's a long way from carrying on my father's oil and gas business—that's what *he* was planning on, I think, when I graduated from law school. Had I done those things, though, the story of Presbyterianism among the Navajos—my doctoral dissertation—might have gone untold, a badly-needed sanctuary in Norfolk, Nebraska, might have gone unbuilt, Christy, Jesse, and Beth would not have come into the world, or would not be the individuals that they are. I never could in any case have been a major league baseball player. God might well have made good use of one more oceanographer, or international mining attorney, or oil producer, or even other Taylor children, but whether by design or default, God's intention is somehow being lived out by my being a Presbyterian minister and occasional historian.

Much more significant in God's greater scheme of things, though, is the story that Genesis tells of how Joseph's life furthered God's purpose of calling and forming and saving a people for himself—a people who would be a light to the nations to declare God's love and judgment and mercy and salvation. God even made use of the evil intentions of Joseph's brothers to lead to a good result. What would have happened to God's people in their famine-plagued homeland if it had not been *Joseph* who was Pharaoh's chief assistant, but someone who was *less* discerning and skillful, or who felt no responsibility for foreigners and no compassion toward them? We can't say, exactly; the Bible indicates that nothing can ultimately stand in the way of God's purpose. God would have found some other avenue. But surely it was Joseph's privilege to have played, even unwittingly, by being sold into slavery, a key role in God's salvation of his beloved creation. In our passage from Romans this morning, Paul tells us that the rejection of Jesus by the Jews ended up fulfilling God's purpose of spreading the gospel to the Gentiles. What the *persecutors* of the Christians intended for *evil*, God was able to use in order to fulfill *his* intentions for *good*.

Anyone who is sensitive to questions about the character of God will recognize that the Bible leads us onto some hazardous ground here. Does the Bible mean to say that a merciful God *wanted* Joseph's brothers to throw him into the pit? Did a *just* God want Jesus to be *unjustly* condemned and executed like a criminal? Did a *saving* God want the gospel to be *rejected* by the Jews? Or does the Bible say that God's purpose is so *sure* that God can use even the fruit of evil intentions to further the certain divine outcome? And short of dealing with *evil* intentions, that God can use the innocent, seemingly neutral little choices that people must make every day to achieve the great divine purpose of restoring creation to its wholeness—whether to cross the street here or there, and so happen to meet someone who needs a word of cheer; whether to attend this college or that, and so happen to meet a teacher who fires a zeal that sets us on a course of career and acquaintances; whether to go out on a date with this person or that, and so happen to fall in love with the sweetheart whom you marry and with whom you have children or can't have children, and whose characteristics and values your children embody?

It was suggested to me a while back that I address in a sermon sometime whether life is simply a matter of chance. A matter of chance? Of course it is—we are free-willed beings, and our casual choices and the circumstances of our environment have much to do with determining how our lives turn out. A matter of chance? Of course it is *not*—no choice that we make, no circumstance of our environment, can thwart the purpose of God to restore the relationship between God and God's creatures which was intended from the beginning of creation. What details of life are *coincidence* and what details of life are *predetermined* remains a divine mystery that no one can fathom, but what remains *un*fathomable is only the *details*. The ruling purpose of God in bringing creation into being, and in giving life to you and to me, is an everlasting love that promises salvation. That everlasting love that promises salvation has been disclosed in countless biblical episodes like that of Joseph and *revisited* in fictional stories like that of Archibald Graham and experienced daily in the true story of your life and my life. That everlasting love that promises salvation has been attested in the ministry, crucifixion, and resurrection of Jesus Christ, and should be proclaimed in everything that his church does. God is *not* capricious. God has a steadfast intention that God is fulfilling, no matter how many possible scenarios God must consider. And isn't it good news that the future of all things depends not upon what *you* and *I* intend, but upon what *God* intends?

Twenty-first Sunday in Ordinary Time

Spanish Springs Presbyterian Church, Sparks, Nevada

August 21, 2011

Exodus 1:8—2:10
Romans 12:1–8
Matthew 16:13–20

"Testaments to Freedom"

A few years ago, I received a letter in the mail here at our street address, which appears in the telephone book, threatening me with eternal damnation if I ever preached on a text from the Old Testament. Jesus Christ, the letter declared, has made the Old Testament irrelevant. "John," as the letter was signed, provided no return address, of course. But, then, neither did the "John" who wrote the three short letters in the New Testament, nor the "John" who wrote Revelation, also in the form of a letter. But I think that this modern "John," who claimed to speak for God with every bit as much authority as did those earlier writers of that name, should have reflected on the fact that Jesus seems to have been not at all reluctant to quote the Old Testament, nor was Matthew, nor was Paul, all of whom the compilers of the *New* Testament pretty clearly thought spoke on God's behalf.

Indeed, for two thousand years, the church has maintained that one can only understand the importance of Jesus Christ by referring back to the Old Testament. The great themes of the Old Testament are fundamental to perceiving how Christ demonstrated and fulfilled the will of God. And Christ's ministry and his commission to his church can only be fully appreciated by considering the history of the *Jews*, including the commandments set forth in their scriptures and the proclamations of their prophets. Indeed, *Matthew*, according to surveys the most beloved of the Gospels, repeatedly draws upon incidents in the life and ministry of the person whom the Jews regard as the *greatest* Old Testament prophet, Moses, in order to convey the story of Jesus. It is in Matthew, for instance, that we learn that Jesus was threatened as an infant by the king of Israel and so was spirited off to Egypt for safety, to emerge from there some time later back into the promised land, rather like Moses was threatened as an infant by the king of Egypt and later emerged from there to lead God's people back to the promised land. In both cases, the kings ordered that all male infants be slaughtered. It is in Matthew that Jesus delivered, by common count, ten axioms for living a blessed life, and did so from a mountainside, reminiscent of how Moses delivered the Ten Commandments that he had received while on a mountain. And, of course, there is the way that Moses, in freeing his people from slavery in Egypt, prefigured Jesus' ministry of setting people free from the slavery of sin and the *effects* of sin—their own sins and the sins of others.

And then there is the way in which Jesus, in *all* of the Gospels, received and associated with and blessed the despised and the marginalized—indeed, one might almost say that that was at the root of why he was arrested and crucified. It was a despised and marginalized population of foreign slaves that Moses championed and led out of slavery. The term "Hebrews," used often in the Bible to identify the descendants of Abraham and Sarah, is a word that actually appears in many different Near Eastern languages and cultures to refer to *any* group of marginalized people who have no social standing and who are feared or excluded or despised. In his own ministry, Jesus, many hundreds of years after the exodus, showed a special concern for such people, anyone who suffered oppression and indignity at the hands of others, including, ironically, those who suffered oppression and indignity at the hands of the very people who traced their ancestry back to those who had *themselves* been oppressed and treated with indignity once upon a time in Egypt—Jews mistreating "Hebrews." For that reason if for no other, the Old Testament story of Moses, at least, is one of great importance for Christians ancient and modern.

It is a story that arises out of a situation as relevant as today's headlines. A foreign people whose presence was once welcome in a more hospitable age came to be feared and despised as they grew in numbers within the land of Egypt. But rather than deport them, the powers in control of the police and the economy decided to put them to work at the jobs the Egyptians themselves did not want to do for wages they would have turned their noses up at. Ironically, the Hebrews were set to the task of building huge storehouses, symbols of the fertility of the land of the Egyptians and the economic wealth of the Egyptians whose *own* women were *not* fertile—at least not as fertile as the *Hebrew* women—and whose population would have *starved* some generations earlier had it not been for the prophetic dreams and managerial skills of a *Hebrew* named Joseph. But in the prejudice of the moment, the Egyptians and their leaders seem to have forgotten how much they owed to these people whom they now regarded as an enemy within. "Come," said the politician, "let us deal shrewdly with them, or they will increase and, in the event of war, join our enemies and fight against us and escape from the land" (Exod 1:10).

Pharaoh at least discerned that, *without* the Hebrews, the economy would collapse. He hit upon the counterproductive plan, so clearly nonsensical in hindsight but probably quite popular at the time, of treating the nation's workforce unjustly with the expectation that they would give birth to fewer children. That, naturally, would have meant that the cheap workforce, so necessary to the economy, would *shrink*. "The Egyptians became ruthless in imposing tasks on the Israelites, and made their lives bitter with hard service in mortar and brick and in every kind of field labor. They were ruthless in all the tasks that they imposed on them" (1:13–14). And finally, when, *despite* their hard life, the Hebrews continued to produce *more* and *more* children while the native Egyptians apparently continued to produce *fewer* and *fewer*, the king of Egypt ordered the Hebrew midwives to kill the newborn little Israelite boys. "Every boy that is born to the Hebrews you shall throw into the Nile" (1:22), Pharaoh ordered. And so, what had always been Egypt's ribbon of life, the Nile, became Egypt's lash of death.

The little boy Moses was put into the Nile, too, in yet another instance of irony, but by his *mother* and in a *basket* as a way that he might be *saved* by means of the river. The word for "basket" here is the same word used for "ark" in Genesis, where the family of Noah and all of the menagerie were saved by means of the water that was otherwise an instrument of destruction. And when the daughter of the king spied the basket and rescued the baby and entrusted it to a Hebrew woman for nursing—who turned out to be Moses' own mother—he grew safe among his people until his mother returned him, now past the age of nursing, to the princess, who raised him in Pharaoh's household. When, as a young man, Moses "saw an Egyptian beating a Hebrew, one of his kinsfolk" (2:11), he killed the Egyptian out of rage at the injustice, and his life's work as a reluctant liberator was fixed.

As one commentator has recently noted, inasmuch as Exodus says that the king was reacting to the increase not of the Israelites, specifically, but the more generic "Hebrews," the issue probably wasn't so much the foreigners' religion or their ethnicity, but their social class.[1] We have here an instance of the "haves" being alarmed by the presence and increase of the "have-nots." Doubtless, the fact that these people were immigrants made them an

---

1. Brueggemann, "Book of Exodus," 695.

easier target, as immigrants have always been and continue to be convenient scapegoats whenever politicians and others want to find an excuse to build popular resentment and divert popular attention. And, as it often does, that quickness to blame led the king to adopt a policy that would have actually made the situation worse. The whole episode about Joseph—of whom the new king was ignorant—demonstrated the importance of the storehouses; they were a necessary hedge against the famine that had once threatened Egypt so severely and might do so again. By refusing to carry out the king's command, the Hebrew midwives, fearing God more than they feared Pharaoh, were *actually* doing what was necessary to prevent Egypt from suffering economic disaster. But Pharaoh's fear and hatred of the fertile and productive Hebrews blinded him to the contradictions of his program of murdering the next generation of cheap labor, on the one hand, and his anxiety to prevent the escape of his current workforce, on the other.

The descendants of Abraham and Sarah, of course, were doing what God had instructed human beings to do way back in the beginning—be fruitful and multiply—so, clearly, what Pharaoh was doing was opposing the will of God, unwittingly setting himself up as an authority who was in *competition* with God. But well below the radar screen, so to speak, of Pharaoh's inflated sense of self-importance, God was quietly at work among the humble faithful working out the divine purpose of salvation, raising up the liberator of his oppressed people in the very household, right under the nose, of the oppressor! And the very things that the oppressor did to increase the injustice on his workers only had the effect of hastening the economic disaster that he had set out to prevent—the departure from Egypt of all that cheap labor and, incidentally, the death of all the Egyptians' firstborn, reminiscent of how Pharaoh had ordered the death of the *Hebrew* infants and as Herod centuries later, in Matthew, ordered the death of the infants in and around *Bethlehem* and as Hitler later ordered the death of *Jewish* children, along with their parents, and the death of *others* deemed "outsiders" in order to prevent their increase in a way that, had Germany won the war, would certainly have meant economic disorder. For when nations adopt the ways of empire—accumulation and coercion—and their leaders set themselves over against the will and purpose of God, there can never be a good outcome. And when nations and their leaders come to regard human beings as both tools of production and wealth, on the one hand, but also nuisances and liabilities, on the other, they are setting themselves over against the ministry and teaching of Jesus Christ.

When the humble poor of ancient times heard the Bible, when black slaves in nineteenth-century America heard it, when campesinos in El Salvador and Nicaragua and Guatemala heard it, and began to think about the ways that the Old and New Testaments link God's works of blessing and liberating the poor and the despised and the foreigner and the oppressed, and the liberating gospel of Jesus Christ and the liberating prophecies of Isaiah and Amos and Joel and the liberating miracles worked through the words and actions of Moses, they reached the same inevitable conclusion of which Mary, pregnant with Jesus, sang when Elizabeth greeted her as the mother of the Son of God:

> My soul magnifies the Lord,
> and my spirit rejoices in God my Savior. . . .
> He was shown strength with his arm;
> he has scattered the proud in the thoughts of their hearts.
> He has brought down the powerful from their thrones,
> and lifted up the lowly;
> he has filled the hungry with good things,
> and sent the rich away empty.
> He has helped his servant Israel,
> in remembrance of his mercy,
> according to the promise he made to our ancestors,
> to Abraham and to his descendants forever.
> (Luke 1:46b-47, 51-55)

"I have observed the misery of my people who are in Egypt," God said to Moses from a burning bush; "I have heard their cry on account of their taskmasters. Indeed, I know their sufferings and I have come down to deliver them from the Egyptians, and to bring them up out of that land to a good and broad land, a land flowing with milk and honey" (Exod 3:7-8).

What does the Old Testament have to do with people who have pledged their loyalty and obedience to the one whom the New Testament testifies is the Messiah, the Son of the living God? Why are stories of freedom from slavery and dignity for the despised outcast significant for the church to which has been given the keys of the kingdom of heaven so that whatever it binds on earth will be bound in heaven and whatever it looses on earth will be loosed in heaven? Might it not all have something to do with what it means to acknowledge Jesus Christ as Savior, and what it means to be his obedient disciple?

Twenty-second Sunday in Ordinary Time

Spanish Springs Presbyterian Church, Sparks, Nevada

August 28, 2011

Exodus 3:1–15
Romans 12:9–21
Matthew 16:21–28

"On Holy Ground"

When Martin Luther, then a young Augustinian priest, said his first mass, he took his place before the altar and began to recite the phrases that he had heard so many times but had never himself been qualified to speak. It was all going fairly well, it seems, until he came to the words, "We offer unto thee, the living, the true, the eternal God." He later wrote about his experience: "At these words I was utterly stupefied and terror-stricken. I thought to myself, 'With what tongue shall I address such Majesty, seeing that all men ought to tremble in the presence of even an earthly prince? Who am I that I should lift up mine eyes or raise my hands to the divine Majesty? The angels surround him. At his nod the earth trembles. And shall I, a miserable little pygmy, say, "I want this, I ask for that"? For I am dust and ashes and full of sin and I am speaking to the living, eternal and the true God.'"[1] The great church historian and biographer of Luther, Roland Bainton, wrote about this first mass said by the young monk who had entered the monastery a few years before after being knocked to the ground by a flash of lightning: "The terror of the Holy, the horror of Infinitude, smote him like a new lightning bolt, and only through a fearful restraint could he hold himself at the altar to the end."[2]

---

1. Quoted at Bainton, *Here I Stand*, 41.
2. Bainton, *Here I Stand*, 41.

Luther's early understanding of God may indeed have been, as Roland Bainton commented, a reaction of primitive religion, a fear of God as being a malevolent deity, essentially an enemy of humankind. But his disquiet at the thought of handling the mysteries of God was augmented by a sense of his own smallness in the universe, and his imperfection, a sinner. Martin Luther later came to appreciate better Jesus Christ as the one through whose sacrifice and grace he need no longer cower in terror of the wrath of God. But that just meant that God was all the *more* worthy of whatever respectful honor we human beings can show to God, grateful for our daily bread, grateful for our eternal salvation—honor given not just in *words*, of course, but in *deeds*, not just bending our *knee* before God's *altar*, but bending our *desires* to match God's *will*.

Nearly five centuries after Martin Luther, very few people seem to tremble anymore at the thought of being in the presence of God in worship. As I've commented elsewhere, we hear the word "awesome" used to describe God a lot these days, but in the mouths of pastors whose training was in the para-church mold, it seems to have pretty much lost its original meaning. And, for whatever reason, the relationship captured in the hymn title "What a Friend We Have in Jesus" is regarded by a lot of people as being more in the vein of "What a *Pal* We Have in Jesus" . . . dude. And when *that* happens, the cost of our salvation quickly becomes devalued, Christ's claim on our life becomes negotiable, and the good *news* is in danger of being interpreted as simply good *advice*.

In her book *Teaching a Stone to Talk*, essayist Annie Dillard wrote something that has been quoted many times since by people who are alarmed at the state of worship in contemporary Western Christianity:

> On the whole, I do not find Christians, outside of the catacombs, sufficiently sensible of conditions. Does anyone have the foggiest idea what sort of power we so blithely invoke? Or, as I suspect, does no one believe a word of it? The churches are children playing on the floor with their chemistry sets, mixing up a batch of TNT to kill a Sunday morning. It is madness to wear ladies' straw hats and velvet hats to church; we should all be wearing crash helmets. Ushers should issue life preservers and signal flares; they should lash us to our pews. For the sleeping god may wake someday to take offense, or the waking god may draw us out to where we can never return.[3]

To put it another way, does anyone here really expect to encounter the living God in worship this morning—the God who made the world and everything

---

3. Dillard, *Teaching a Stone*, 52–53.

that is in it, the God who is powerful enough to destroy all of creation in an instant but who is, so far at least, gracious enough not to do so, the God whom the Bible describes as being wrapped in an impenetrable cloud of smoke and who speaks through fire, the God who gives as the divine name a word that is saturated with mystery and ambiguity and inscrutability, the God who then provides as a self-portrait a baby lying humbly in a feeding trough and a condemned young adult hanging bloody on a cross?

The God of the *New* Testament, Christians believe, is the same God testified to in the *Old* Testament. The divine purpose has not changed. Nor has the divine personality. In one of the best-known passages of scripture, a shepherd tending his father-in-law's flock, and who happened to be a recent fugitive from the threats of a very human being, was grazing his sheep in the shadow of Mount Horeb, which in other passages of the Bible is called Mount Sinai. His attention was caught by a bush that was blazing with fire, but was not burning up. The shepherd said,

> "I must turn aside and look at this great sight, and see why the bush is not burned up." When the Lord saw that he had turned aside to see, God called to him out of the bush, "Moses, Moses!" And he said, "Here I am." Then he said, "Come no closer! Remove the sandals from your feet, for the place on which you are standing is holy ground." He said further, "I am the God of your father, the God of Abraham, the God of Isaac, and the God of Jacob." And Moses hid his face, for he was afraid to look at God.
>
> Then the Lord said, "I have observed the misery of my people who are in Egypt; I have heard their cry on account of their taskmasters. Indeed, I know their sufferings, and I have come down to deliver them from the Egyptians, and to bring them up out of that land to a good and broad land. . . . The cry of the Israelites has now come to me; I have also seen how the Egyptians oppress them. So come, I will send you to Pharaoh to bring my people, the Israelites, out of Egypt." (Exod 3:3–10)

And when Moses expressed doubt that the king of Egypt would listen to him so that indeed he could lead the Israelites out of their bondage, God said, "I will be with you; and this shall be the sign for you that it is I who sent you: when you have brought the people out of Egypt, you shall worship God on this mountain" (3:12)—that is, on the holy ground where Moses had discovered himself to be in the presence of God.

And all through the remainder of the books of Moses and, indeed, all through the Old Testament, when people acknowledge themselves to be in the presence of God, there is awe, there is mystery, there is respect, there is reverence. God speaks. People listen. God directs. People respond. The prophet Isaiah fears for his life, realizing that, in the temple, he is standing in the presence of God. And in the New Testament, the blind and the lame and the sick fall to their knees before Jesus in fearful wonder and boundless gratitude for being healed, conscious that, in *his* presence, they must, in fact, be in the presence of *God*. Do *our* attitudes, does *our* demeanor, do *our* expectations as we come into this place, indicate that *we* believe *ourselves* to be in the presence of God? Do we recognize that *we* are standing on holy ground? Are we aware of the awesome *power* of the one we have come here to worship? Are we aware of the profound *commitment* to which God in Christ is calling us?

Peter had probably been infused with a sense of euphoria when he broke through all human assessments of Jesus and proclaimed his bold spiritual insight, "You are the Messiah, the Son of the living God" (Matt 16:16). Mountaintop experiences always impressed him; surely this was one of those, not unlike youth mega-rallies with the attendant music and testimonies. But the mood changed dramatically when the reality of what that meant for *Jesus* became clear, *and* what that required of his *followers*. "Jesus began to show his disciples that he must go to Jerusalem and undergo great suffering at the hands of the elders and chief priests and scribes, and be killed, and on the third day be raised" (16:21). Peter objected—surely that wasn't what being the Son of God could be about. But the news got even more disturbing. "Then Jesus told his disciples, 'If any want to become my followers, let them deny themselves and take up their cross and follow me. For those who want to save their life will lose it, and those who lose their life for my sake will find it'" (16:24–25). Jesus had just been talking about his own death. Now, the disciples must have understood, he was talking about *theirs*, as a result of faithfulness to him.

"It is madness to wear ladies' straw hats and velvet hats to church," Annie Dillard writes; "we should be wearing crash helmets. Ushers should issue life preservers and signal flares; they should lash us to our pews."[4] Short of martyrdom, even, the cost of being a disciple is great, will take us down roads we would prefer not to travel, will require of us sacrifices we would rather not make. That is not good news for a lot of people, even for a lot of people in a lot of Christian churches today that seldom talk about the discomfort of being a genuine disciple of Jesus Christ, the suffering it will undoubtedly entail: "Let love be genuine; hate what is evil, hold fast to what is good; love one another with mutual affection; outdo one another in showing honor. Do not lag in zeal, be ardent in spirit, serve the Lord. Rejoice in

---

4. Dillard, *Teaching a Stone*, 52.

hope, be patient in suffering, persevere in prayer. Contribute to the needs of the saints; extend hospitality to strangers" (Rom 12:9–13).

That is what this God requires, who has called us to obedience in Jesus Christ. But it gets even more rigorous, distances us even more from the wisdom and values of the world.

> Bless those who persecute you; bless and do not curse them. Rejoice with those who rejoice, weep with those who weep. Live in harmony with one another; do not be haughty, but associate with the lowly; do not claim to be wiser than you are. Do not repay anyone evil for evil, but take thought for what is noble in the sight of all. If it is possible, so far as depends on you, live peaceably with all. Beloved, never avenge yourselves, but leave room for the wrath of God. . . . No, "if your enemies are hungry, feed them; if they are thirsty, give them something to drink. . . ." Do not be overcome by evil, but overcome evil with good. (12:14–21)

Can our worship carry such freight? Does our music, do our prayers, does the preaching present honestly what it means to be a person of God, a follower of Christ, and does it all sound clearly the call to faithful discipleship?

There is great joy in being in the presence of God. There is great joy in being a follower of Jesus Christ. But the joy lies beyond and through the portals of reverent fear of God and sober assessment of Christ's demands. To find oneself on holy ground is to find oneself utterly vulnerable, to acknowledge oneself as utterly dependent, to confess oneself a miserable sinner, to lay aside all pretended defenses, to place oneself at the mercy of the Creator of all things, to be willing to do all that his Son commands, which means, among other things, always setting aside one's own desires, preferences, tastes, and agendas, even, perhaps, the agenda of living a long and happy and comfortable and respectable life. But, after all, what will it profit them if they gain the whole world but forfeit their soul?

Moses, fully understanding that it was indeed holy ground on which he stood, discovered that, in the full light of the burning bush, he could not avoid the urgency of God's command. Every excuse he raised, every evasion he proposed, God exposed and knocked down. For the need to free oppressed people from their *bondage* was urgent. "So come," God said, "I will send you to Pharaoh to bring my people, the Israelites, out of Egypt" (Exod 3:10). Yes, Moses should have donned a crash helmet before he turned aside from his peaceful, stress-free afternoon with the sheep to investigate the strange wonder of the bush that was ablaze but not reduced to cinders.

For he was about to learn just how dangerous it is to be standing on holy ground—to be in the presence of the living God who insists on faithfulness, on obedience, and on justice and mercy and dignity.

That raises some serious questions about worship—questions that a congregation and its leaders should constantly ask themselves, the basis on which their worship should continually be gauged and reformed and renewed. Is it just a time for gathering with friends and like-minded people? Or is it an experience of being in the presence of the God who *makes* us a people? Is it an occasion for hearing some nice thoughts *about* God, or is it a time for intentionally listening for God speaking *to* us? Is it something that is supposed to help us feel *good* about ourselves, or is it something that, in the radiance of the bush that is burning and the shadow of the cross on which Jesus was put to death, should cause us to see ourselves and the world around us *honestly*, as *God* sees? Is it an opportunity for spiritual self-indulgence, perhaps picking up a suggestion here or there about how to make life easier and more pleasant, or is it an experience of commitment to making a sacrificial offering of ourselves, indeed our whole life, to the lordship of Jesus Christ, the very Word of God?

Paradoxically, the only way to a life of profound joy and abiding peace and eternal happiness is to set foot on holy ground, allowing the Word of God to search our souls, searing, cleansing, claiming. It does not mean that we can't be people of laughter, light-hearted and affectionate. Quite the contrary—it makes laughter pure, it enables us to go into the world unburdened, it binds us in relationships that transcend even death. But all of that is possible only because of the sober knowledge that the ground on which we are standing when we come together to worship is holy, for we are in the awesome presence of the living God.

Twenty-third Sunday in Ordinary Time
Spanish Springs Presbyterian Church, Sparks, Nevada

September 8, 2002

Exodus 12:1–14
Romans 13:8–14
Matthew 18:15–20

"Slaves No More"

On July 4, like many Americans, I enjoy watching fireworks displays in celebration of our independence. July 4, 1776, is, of course, the date on which the Declaration of Independence was approved by the Continental Congress. But was that really the day of America's freedom? The Revolutionary War went on for more than five years after July 4, 1776. France—the first nation to recognize the United States as an independent state—did not do so until December 17, 1777. Lord Cornwallis did not surrender at Yorktown until October 19, 1781. The British cabinet did not agree to acknowledge American independence until March 1782, and did not sign a preliminary peace treaty until November 30, 1782. The final Treaty of Paris wasn't signed until September 3, 1783, and it wasn't ratified by the American Congress until January 14, 1784. So when did the people of the United States become free?

Let me muddy the waters a little more. President Lincoln didn't sign the Emancipation Proclamation until January 1, 1863, officially freeing the slaves in the Confederacy. That news didn't reach African Americans in Texas until June 19, 1865—*months* after Appomattox. President Johnson signed the Civil Rights Act in the summer of 1964. The Voting Rights Act wasn't passed until the summer of 1965. When did Americans become free?

A week from next Saturday, we will have the opportunity to hear about Cornelia Ten Boom—"Corrie"—a remarkable person from a remarkable family who sheltered Jews in their house in Haarlem in the Netherlands during the Nazi occupation, and who was interned first in a prison and then in a concentration camp, but who never gave up hope, never abandoned the God who never abandoned *her*, refused to let hatred become her master despite every cruelty and indignity, never once returned evil for the monstrous evil that was done to her, to her family, to the people around her. Corrie Ten Boom's book, *The Hiding Place*, and the movie that was made from it, reveal that she, in fact, was one of the *few* persons in the concentration camp who were *free*—freer, really, than the guards and the wardens who were uncritically following orders, and who would have been shot for doing what was humane, what was fair, what was right.

Perhaps freedom is much more than a matter of treaties and constitutions. If so, then *slavery* can just as much be the condition of someone in the United States as in North Korea. Perhaps freedom is a matter of the spirit. If so, then *slavery* is a matter of the spirit, as well. Perhaps freedom is the soul's acknowledgment that the only one with *ultimate* power over us is loving and generous and just, and will sustain us through every terror and recompense us for every loss. If so, then slavery is the soul's thralldom to any pretentious authority that is not loving and not generous and not just, and will let us down when our soul is in jeopardy. Perhaps freedom is being always prepared to flee captivity at a moment's notice, unencumbered by excess baggage and unworthy loyalties. If so, then *slavery* is whatever weighs us down in life and causes us to hazard missing opportunities to be the people we were created to be, the opportunities to enjoy the gifts of God as they come our way, the freedom from false hopes and false allegiances to share those gifts fully with others, including the gift of forgiveness.

To the degree that Americans lived as free people even *before* other nations recognized our independence, July 4, 1776, was indeed our independence day. To the degree that black people working in the fields did not return hatred for their degradation, *they* were freer than their *masters*. And even before they escaped Pharaoh's army through the waters of the Red Sea, the Israelites who trusted the redeeming purpose of God, who remembered the covenant God made with Abraham, who acted upon the promise God made to Moses, who smeared their doorposts with the blood of a lamb and baked bread without leaven and dressed themselves for a journey out of captivity, were already free from the power of tyranny, the rod of oppression, the pain and suffering of slavery. And, even before the kingdom of God is a full reality in *our* world, those who taste the bread of heaven and the cup of blessing are free from slavery to the passions and prejudices and pretensions of the world and its powers and principalities. "The LORD said to Moses and Aaron in the land of Egypt: This month shall mark for you the beginning of months" (Exod 12:1–2a)—like a new beginning for their lives.

> Tell the whole congregation of Israel that on the tenth of this month they are to take a lamb for each family, a lamb for each household. . . . You shall keep it until the fourteenth day of this month; then the whole assembled congregation of Israel shall slaughter it at twilight. They shall take some of the blood and put it on the two doorposts and the lintel of the houses in which they eat it. . . . You shall let none of it remain until the morning. . . . This is how you shall eat it: your loins girded, your sandals on your feet, and your staff in your hand; and you shall eat it hurriedly. It is the Passover of the LORD. For I will pass through the land of Egypt that night, and I will strike down every first-born in the land of Egypt. . . . The blood shall be a sign for you on the houses where you live: when I see the blood, I will pass over you, and no plague shall destroy you when I strike the land of Egypt.
> This day shall be a day of remembrance for you. You shall celebrate it as a festival to the LORD; throughout your generations you shall observe it as a perpetual ordinance. (Exod 12:3, 6–7, 10a, 11–12a, 13–14)

For a long time, we Americans had seemed protected from the hateful violence of the rest of the world. At least for the Europeans who migrated to these shores, two oceans were like blood on the doorposts, a protection against the death and destruction that otherwise seemed to cycle around the planet. Two world wars certainly had an impact *here*, but they were *fought* "over there." Even that other catastrophic foreign attack on American soil didn't really seem like American soil at the time—the news of Pearl Harbor must have sent a lot of Americans scrambling for maps to find out just exactly where Hawaii *was*. But the tragedy of September 11, 2001, unfolded on our television screens, live and in color. It destroyed skylines we knew. It scarred monuments to our security. It killed people like us—mothers, fathers, children, brothers, sisters, grandparents, aunts, uncles, cousins, friends. The routine of business and busy-ness halted, as we were shocked not only at *what* happened, but shocked that it *could* happen. And *all* of us, briefly at least, reconsidered what is truly precious to us. And *some* of us, briefly at least, reconsidered the meaning of security—or where true security lies. And a *few* of us, briefly at least, amid the speeches about assaults on our freedoms, pondered the responsibilities that freedom imposes. And it is just possible that, in the first hours and days of our grim national sorrow, when we shared a grief, when we wept for other people's loss, when we embraced each other across lines of color and race and religion, when we forgot about making money and making a reputation, when we regarded our families and friends and public servants and community institutions with renewed appreciation, when we turned to the God who made heaven and earth, our only sure hope and strong defender, our nation was more free than it had ever been. Our greatest challenge as a nation now remains not to surrender, out of fear, out of hatred, out of pride, those very freedoms and convictions of equality for which our nation stands.

Slavery was a common fact of life in the world in which the apostle Paul lived. There were slaves in the early church. There were slave *owners* in the early church. And so it was natural that Paul sometimes spoke about life *in* Jesus Christ and life *apart* from Jesus Christ in terms of freedom and slavery—freedom from anything that would keep us from responding to Christ, freedom from anything that would keep us from being ready for Christ's return, freedom from anything that would make us once again slaves, now that Christ had *freed* us from the burden of the law, freed us from the power of sin, freed us from the finality of death, freed us from pride, freed us from fear, freed us from hatred, freed us from selfishness, freed us from our possessions, freed us from anxiety. The Christian, Paul declared, was to be a slave no more; and then, he admonished slaves to be subject to their masters. Now, what kind of double-talk is that?

I doubt that Paul *approved* of the institution of slavery. He believed sincerely that God had brought the Israelites up out of bondage in Egypt. But he surely recognized that slavery is not *only*, not even *primarily*, a matter of people being bought and sold, subject to the whim of another. "Owe no one anything"—not money, not loyalty or allegiance or obedience, even— "except to *love* one another; for the one who loves another has *fulfilled* the law" (Rom 13:8). The love that Christ commands makes us all servants of one another, all bound to work for the well-being of one another, all living for the sake of one another. "The commandments, 'You shall not commit adultery; You shall not murder; You shall not steal; You shall not covet'; and any other commandment, are summed up in this word, 'Love your neighbor as yourself.' Love does no wrong to a neighbor; therefore, love is the fulfilling of the law" (13:9–10). The freedom Christ has won for us on the cross releases us from slavery to *anyone*, and frees us for love active in deeds of kindness and generosity and mercy toward *everyone*. God's will, signaled and accomplished in the exodus from Egypt, is that no one should anymore be a slave, treated as less than the image of God in which each person was created. God's will, signaled and accomplished in the cross of Jesus, is that no one is anymore a slave to sin and death, in *bondage* to sin and death, in bondage to our possessions or our lusts or our fears, separated from God by our *own* faithlessness or *anyone else's*. Drunkenness, debauchery, licentiousness, quarreling, jealousy—Paul lists some of the signs that people are still in bondage. You are *free*, Paul told the early Christians, and his words are still true. Live in freedom. Don't ever turn back to the dungeons. Don't ever become nostalgic for your chains. Don't ever doubt that Christ lives within you, that God will provide for you. Don't ever give in to the fear and jealousy and hatred that would enslave you. You are in Christ Jesus. You are slaves no more. You are in Christ Jesus. You are the servants of everyone. You are in Christ Jesus. You belong to no human being. You are in Christ Jesus. You belong to God, and in God is your perfect freedom.

On that first Passover night long ago, I can well imagine that it would have been easy to give in to doubt—in spite of the prospect of freedom, to scoff at Moses' instructions and make battle plans instead, or to be paralyzed by fear into doing nothing at all. But they trusted in God's promise. They expected God's dependability. They did not enslave themselves to fear. They did not trade in their hope for *tomorrow's blessings* on the certainty of *today's misery*. They shed everything that was unnecessary, and put themselves in the hands of God. They ate the bread, and they tasted the freedom that was already theirs even while they were still in Pharaoh's Egypt.

Take, eat. This is the token of our salvation—Christ's body broken for us, Christ's blood shed for us, the taste of the kingdom of God which already is, but is not yet. *Our* freedom has already been won in the death and resurrection of Christ, so that we can obey the commandment to love our neighbor as ourself. We are slaves no more, but willing and faithful servants of God through the Master, Jesus Christ our Lord.

Twenty-fourth Sunday in Ordinary Time
Spanish Springs Presbyterian Church, Sparks, Nevada
September 15, 2002

Exodus 14:19–31
Romans 14:1–12
Matthew 18:21–35

"The Way God Works"

"If God wanted people to stop fighting wars," a crusty old church member once said, "he'd do something to stop them." "If God didn't want those people to starve," another church member once said, "God would do something to feed them." "If God wanted Amy to live," yet another church member once said, "God would have healed her." We've all heard people say such things. We've heard them on the news. I've even heard a few of them from members of some of the churches *I've* served. It's a common form of piety, I guess, in their own minds, an affirmation of God's power and sovereignty. But of course, it isn't much comfort to grieving relatives to be told that the death of their loved one was simply God's will. And to lay at God's feet wars and famines and all sorts of misery that the devil revels in not only begs questions about God's goodness, but also relieves us human beings of any responsibility for whatever happens in the world.

The topic of why God allows suffering in the world is one that has engaged a lot of philosophers and theologians over the centuries, one that has been tackled in hundreds or thousands of books, most of them offering, frankly, pretty unconvincing explanations. The Bible itself doesn't provide any single, simple reason, though over and over it affirms God's goodness and God's power and God's sovereignty, and speaks of how the forces of nature are at God's command, and how God uses kings and emperors to work God's will, often unwittingly. The Bible *does* give Jesus' instruction to turn the other cheek, to forgive as often as we are wronged, seventy-seven times or even seventy times seven, to heal the sick, to feed the hungry, to love our neighbor, even if our neighbor has been our enemy, by doing that person good and not evil. I'm not going to try to answer the question of suffering to everyone's satisfaction this morning, except to say that the Bible offers *no* testimony that every case of suffering or pain or death or destruction is the will of God, or that any particular disease is God's will, or that any particular incident of famine or pestilence or plague is God's will.

The Bible *does*, though, provide a witness of *faith* that God is powerfully at work in the world, in and through the events of history and in and through the forces of nature and in and through the everyday decisions and activities of people like you and me, to achieve the divine purpose. God is bringing creation to its completion. God is achieving the divine purpose of wholeness. God is bringing about the relationship of perfect harmony and fellowship that God *intended* and *still* intends for the world God loves so much. One such evidence of this is the event that has been at the heart of the testimony of the people of God from very ancient times—indeed, it is the event that formed the consciousness of the people of God as specially God's own. That is the liberation of the descendants of Abraham and Sarah from Egypt through the miracle of the parting of the waters of the Red Sea. And it is instructive for us to examine closely what the Bible has to say about this mighty act of God, to reclaim it from Cecil B. DeMille and bring its lesson into modern times.

For one thing, Israel's escape from Egypt shows that God is adaptable to the events of human history. Once upon a time, a young man, the bearer of God's promise first made to Abraham and Sarah—their great-grandson, in fact—was sold by his jealous brothers as a slave to some passing traders. In a twist that seemed to spell the *end* of God's plan, the boy was taken into Egypt. There, through the use of the same power of dreams that had gotten him into trouble with his brothers, he earned Pharaoh's favor by predicting a great famine, and then telling Pharaoh how to prepare for it. Because of Joseph's counsel, Egypt stockpiled tons of food to see its people through years when all the rest of the region went hungry. That got the attention of Joseph's father and brothers back home, who came down to Egypt seeking food. You know the story of how, eventually, Joseph revealed his identity to his brothers and showed them *mercy* rather than *revenge*, and how Pharaoh invited the whole family to come down into Egypt, to settle in the land of Goshen, where they grew in numbers and prosperity.

But God had promised Abraham and Sarah their ancestors that *Canaan* was to be their home. In their new home of plenty and satisfaction, *God's* destination had been forgotten. But then came along a pharaoh who had not known Joseph and had no love for the Hebrews, who regarded them as unwelcome and prolific aliens who looked like they were going to become more numerous than the native people, a threat to the Egyptian way of life, dressing different, speaking a foreign language in their homes, eating funny food. So the Egyptians enslaved the Hebrews, made them their laborers, to build their great warehouses and grand monuments, and treated them harshly and with contempt.

In the meantime, a little Hebrew boy was born in the normal way, and he was saved from an edict of death by the subterfuge of a Hebrew mother acting with a mother's love and the whim of an Egyptian princess acting with simple compassion and was raised right under Pharaoh's own nose in the lap of luxury. But when he grew up, he saw the oppression of the Hebrews and he killed one of their taskmasters and fled to escape punishment for the murder—a common fugitive. While tending his father-in-law's sheep one day as an ordinary shepherd, he was summoned by God to lead the Israelites out of Egypt, out of slavery, to the land that God had promised them. Reluctantly, Moses went to Pharaoh and demanded that he let the Israelites go free, but Pharaoh would not comply, until after a miraculous series of natural disasters.

Finally, Pharaoh gave in, but then he changed his mind. And as the Israelites were starting their journey to freedom, all of them, Pharaoh and his soldiers and cavalry came up behind them. The people panicked, and turned on Moses. "Was it because there were no graves in Egypt that you have taken us away to die in the wilderness?" (Exod 14:11). "Then the LORD said to Moses, 'Why do you cry out to me? Tell the Israelites to go forward. But *you* lift up your staff, and stretch out your hand over the sea and divide it, that the Israelites may go into the sea on dry ground. Then I will harden the hearts of the Egyptians so that they will go in after them; and so I will gain glory for myself over Pharaoh and all his army, his chariots, and his chariot drivers. And the Egyptians shall know that I am the LORD'" (14:15-18a).

Did you hear what God said to Moses? It was what *Moses* would do, *as well as* what *God* would do, that would result in God's glory, that would result in the Egyptians knowing the power and purpose of God. "Tell the Israelites to go ahead. Lift up your staff. Stretch out your hand over the sea" (14:15b-16a). God promised to divide the waters so that the Israelites would cross over, and, when the Egyptians saw them doing so, they would pursue them. All through the night, the angel of God was with the Israelites, and a great cloud—did it look like fog?—hid the Israelites from the Egyptians until they came to the seashore. "Then Moses stretched out his hand over the sea. The LORD drove the sea back by a strong east wind all night, and turned the sea into dry land; and the waters were divided" (14:21). So not only the qualities of human leadership in the obedient person of Moses, but also natural phenomena of cloud and wind, joined with God's eternal purpose of salvation to bring about the miracle of the Israelites' deliverance through the Red Sea. The waters formed a wall on either side of their path to freedom.

Just as God had said, the Egyptians pursued them right into the pathway between the waters, "all of Pharaoh's horses, chariots, and chariot drivers" (14:23b). The unarmed and unencumbered and low-tech Israelites walked across the bare seabed, but the heavy, weapon-laden, state-of-the-art army of Pharaoh bogged down in the muck. The Egyptians panicked, as the truth finally dawned on them and they acknowledged God, just as God told Moses they would: "Let us flee from the Israelites, for the Lord is fighting for them against Egypt" (14:25b). Their stratagems, their weapons, their generals—what match were they for the power of God? Pharaoh had obstructed the Israelites' freedom with his stubbornness and hardness of heart, but Pharaoh could not prevent God from achieving the salvation that God purposed. "Then the Lord said to Moses, 'Stretch out your hand over the sea, so that the water may come back upon the Egyptians, upon their chariots and chariot drivers'" (14:26). Again, God employed a human agent to work the divine deliverance.

> So Moses stretched out his hand over the sea, and at dawn the sea returned to its normal depth. As the Egyptians fled before it, the Lord tossed the Egyptians into the sea. The waters returned and covered the chariots and the chariot drivers, the entire army of Pharaoh that had followed them into the sea; not one of them remained. But the Israelites walked on dry ground through the sea. . . .
> *Thus* the Lord saved Israel that day from the Egyptians; and Israel saw the Egyptians dead on the seashore. Israel saw the great work that the Lord did against the Egyptians. So the people feared the Lord and believed in the Lord and in his servant Moses. (14:27–31)

Notice that the Bible recognizes very clearly whose mighty miracle this *was—God's*. And the Bible admits very candidly the way in which God *worked* the miracle—through the faithfulness of *Moses*, through a cloud that was in just the right place at just the right time, through a windstorm that was strong enough to blow back the treacherous waters, *even* through the flinty hatefulness of Pharaoh and the clumsy sophistication of his weaponry, and the natural return of the tides to their normal level. But the fact that it was *God* who was at work, making *use* of all these pieces, to move creation another inch along toward its completion, probably would not even be *apparent* except to the eyes of faith. It is the eyes of faith that see in this episode a mighty saving act of God. Otherwise, it's just a report about a fugitive from justice turned rabble-rouser, a freak typhoon, a brash king seething with such fierce hatred that he followed a very foolish tactic, all happening to coincide in a way that permitted a bunch of scruffy slaves to escape into a desert wilderness where there wasn't any food and water anyway! To the eyes of faith, the scene of the Israelites who had cried out in their misery, now standing silent, safe on the Sinai shore, looking across the water at the bodies of all the dead Egyptian soldiers washed up on the beach opposite, is a powerful statement about how God deals with oppressors, how God preserves God's chosen, how *inevitable* is the outcome once *God* has entered the fray.

It is to ignore the witness of the Bible itself to say that the church should not be involved in politics; God sometimes chooses to work that way. It is to ignore the summons of the Bible itself for people of faith to assume that *they* aren't a part of the solution to social problems; God called on a Moses to raise a people up from their chains. It is to ignore the hope of the Bible itself for anyone to think that God is not, right now, in and through the stories making the headlines of today's newspaper, working a mighty act of salvation, bringing creation closer to the moment of its final redemption.

What miracles of God are being overlooked in our *own* time? Is God completing the salvation of the world by your simple act of bringing a canned food item to church on communion Sunday? Or your feeling the Holy Spirit's nudge to serve a meal to the homeless and spend an evening of friendship with them for the Interfaith Hospitality Network? Could it be your yielding to the suggestion to go through your closet and make a donation to Good Shepherd's Clothes Closet? May it be your summoning the courage to go to a city council meeting and speak out against some injustice or abuse, or perhaps running for a political office *yourself* to bring the convictions of your faith to bear on the public issues of our day? And the sunshine or the rain, the heat or the cold, the calm or the wind that day— who knows but what nature may be joined to your response as instruments working God's miracle? A lot of the people around you will probably not even notice. But the eyes of faith may well detect that God has been at work.

Twenty-fifth Sunday in Ordinary Time
Spanish Springs Presbyterian Church, Sparks, Nevada
September 19, 1999

Exodus 16:2–15
Philippians 1:21–30
Matthew 20:1–16

"God's Economy"

Do you remember any time since the Great Depression when the *economy* was so much in the headlines? Do you remember any time when *money*—making it, and then making *more* of it—so seemed the most important thing in people's lives? From undreamed-of stock market highs to mega-mergers to round-the-clock "e-commerce," everything these days is business, business, business, except it *isn't* so much *business*—at least not in the sense of focusing on better products and helpful services. It's more a matter of greed and power and control, as, in a lot of cases, competition is disappearing and the quality of services is declining, and executive salaries skyrocket while employees are discarded by the thousands. Stock values are unrelated to what is actually being produced; many of the fastest-growing stocks are for companies that have never declared a profit. A lot of it has to do with instant communications and computers and overnight delivery; the technology that was supposed to give us more time for recreation and family togetherness is actually having the effect of forcing more people to work seven days a week and sometimes take on second and even third jobs. We hang on every hint of a trend; some people are even scrutinizing the color of necktie the chairman of the Federal Reserve Board is wearing for a sign of whether interest rates will go up or remain the same. And we, as a society, are swallowing the explanations and falling into line as we play out our roles as producers and consumers, afraid of being left behind in the rush to the newest and biggest and best, frightened that our schools are not preparing our children for their highest earning potential, scared of poverty in our old age, and we can't figure out what's missing from our lives and we can't understand why families are falling apart and we can't explain why everyone seems more materialistic and more tired and more angry. Surprise! We are caught in the very chains of bondage that our *human* dreams of paradise have created.

In Israel of old, there was always a tension between the tempting comforts of a land of milk and honey and the memories of how it was when the people of God were on the move in the wilderness, unencumbered by the burdens of prosperity. I have heard a lot of people speak wistfully about the hard times of the thirties. "We didn't know we were poor," some older Midwesterners have told me, usually the ones who now drive Cadillacs and sit on the corporate boards of banks and go to Florida in the winter. "You don't miss what you've never had." That's true enough when it applies to things like cell phones and computers and Jacuzzis, though it's probably less true when you're talking about the basics of food and shelter. But there's plenty of evidence that affluence can be a seductive goal and a corrosive achievement. Many of you are aware that I collect old 8-millimeter movies; one that I recently showed my children is a Little Rascals film from the late 1920s, about a poor little rich kid, primmed and isolated from other children in his fine home and pampered with many servants. The boy finally discovers the joy of youth when he breaks out of his gilded cage and mixes with children who make their own fun with discarded junk in an abandoned barn. You know what I'm talking about—and you would recognize the irony that the movie was produced by multimillionaires who lived in Hollywood mansions.

For generations, the Israelites had been groaning under their harsh service in Egypt. Finally, the God who observed their misery and heard their cry and knew their sufferings came down to deliver them from the Egyptians, to bring them back into the land that had been promised to Abraham many centuries before, and God appointed Moses to lead the chosen people from slavery to freedom. But freedom, for the Israelites, was always an opportunity to fall into some new sort of enslavement—enslavement to other gods, enslavement to fleshly desires, enslavement to their own pretentious wisdom. After all, there was a sort of *security* in slavery—at least you knew what to expect, and *your* responsibility for the way things were *around* you was pretty limited; what you had no power to change, you really couldn't be held accountable for. In fact, within weeks after Moses led them through the Red Sea out of bondage in Egypt and along their trek through the Sinai toward the promised land, "the whole congregation of the Israelites complained against Moses and Aaron in the wilderness" (Exod 15:2). "We're hungry!" they said. There wasn't a casino buffet in sight—not even a McDonald's. "At least, while we were slaves in Egypt, our taskmasters made sure that we were *fed*. There's not a blade of grass in this desert. Better that we were dead *back there* than hungry *out here* in this God-forsaken wasteland."

Moses and Aaron, of course, were only doing what God had directed them to do. By complaining against God's chosen leaders, the people were really complaining against God, even if they didn't realize it. We can imagine that God was a little chagrined at the ingratitude of the Israelites. They had, after all, benefited from some really first-class miracles. Still, God responded attentively to their grumbling and to the plight of Moses and Aaron. "The Lord said to Moses, 'I am going to rain bread from heaven for you, and each day the people shall go out and gather enough for that day. In that way I will *test* them, whether they will follow my instruction or not. On the sixth day, when they prepare what they bring in, it will be twice as much as they gather on the other days'" (Exod 16:4–5). In other words, they were not to spend their *sabbath* toiling to support themselves.

Moses told the people that God would provide bread to eat every morning, and even meat to eat every evening. And

> in the evening quails came up and covered the camp; and in the morning there was a layer of dew around the camp. When the layer of dew lifted, there on the surface of the wilderness was a fine flaky substance.... Moses said to them, "It is the bread that the Lord has given you to eat. This is what the Lord has commanded: 'Gather as much of it as each of you needs....'" The Israelites did so, some gathering more, some less. But when they measured it... those who gathered *much* had nothing left over, and those who gathered *little* had no shortage; they gathered as much as each of them needed. And Moses said to them, "Let no one leave any of it over until morning."...
> On the sixth day they gathered twice as much food.... When all the leaders of the congregation came and told Moses, he said to them, "This is what the Lord has commanded: 'Tomorrow is a day of solemn rest, a holy sabbath to the Lord.'" (Exod 16:13–19, 22–23a)

Six days the people of God were to work at gathering what the Lord provided, but the seventh day, they were to leave off their labor, trusting that what they had gathered would be sufficient to last through the day of rest, as God had promised. And it was.

Did you catch those words that God said to Moses?—"Each day the people shall go out and gather enough for that day. In that way I will test them, whether they will follow my instruction or not'" (16:4). God wasn't testing them to see whether they would be diligent workers. God was testing them to see whether they would trust God's promises to provide sufficient for their needs. Would they live by faith in God's power and deliverance? Or would they *lack* faith in God's ability and *depend*ability, and start to hoard, start to spend their time, even the sabbath day of rest, stocking up against the hunch that God would in fact prove *un*faithful, that God would prove *un*reliable, that God had brought them out of their well-fed slavery in Egypt just to let them starve in the freedom of the wilderness? In the economy that God established for the people, everyone was to have adequate and no one was to have excess.

The manna was a free gift of God's grace. To spend time grasping for *more* was a sign that the people did not trust God's faithfulness—that they didn't *want* deliverance from their slavery, that they didn't *believe* that God could or would lead them through the wilderness as God had promised. In fact, a few of the Israelites *did* try to store some of the fine, flaky stuff away over night, and it bred worms and became foul—the equivalent of the moths and rust that Jesus spoke of many centuries later in the Sermon on the Mount. The hunger of the Israelites was a *material* crisis over food and drink, but their murmuring and then their hoarding was a *spiritual* crisis over their faith in God. Their anxiety about their present plight even warped their memory about their miserable past, made freedom a revulsion and slavery appealing. They had forgotten their oppression and thought only about the food. Lacking faith in God's trustworthiness, they were willing to make a very poor trade indeed. And that lack of faith in the trustworthiness of God even meant that when God blessed them with *daily bread*, their only thought was how they could get *more*. How could they build a storehouse? How could they amass a surplus? How could they become self-sufficient so that they would not *have* to depend upon God?

Had they forgotten that storing up and hoarding and setting themselves against one another in the competition of grabbing as much as possible were the ways of *Egypt*?—the ways of anxiety and greed and *un*faith? *Israel* was to be *different*. The people of *God* were supposed to *trust* God. This unearned and gracious gift of bread was to be a *break* from Egypt, where food was a reward that had to be earned, and even admired and coveted. The Israelites had been cruelly exploited back there. God had liberated them so that they would be *free* from all of that—free from fear and abuse and anxiety and exploitation. By the grace of God, the bread had a way of being there when it was needed, all through their long wilderness journey of dangers and weariness and discontent—even disobedience. Everyone had enough. It was bread from heaven, given freely to all by the hand of God, not won by competitive snatching from the hand of Pharaoh. It was not bread to be hoarded in a land of death, but bread that was blessed and broken and shared to give the power of life.

Lest we think that the manna in the wilderness is an isolated case, far removed from our sophisticated age of monetary boards and global markets, a quaint story but hardly realistic as a model for the twenty-first century, consider that you and I have been given by Christ the ministry of proclaiming the kingdom of heaven in our own time, and among the many parables that Jesus told about the kingdom of heaven, what it is like, he spoke of a landowner who set out to hire laborers for his vineyard. He went to the employment office early in the morning and made an agreement with some workers to pay them the usual daily wage—an amount equal to the coin known as a denarius—and hired them to bring in his harvest before it spoiled. But he apparently miscalculated, and so he had to go back to the employment office a little later in the morning, and hire some additional day laborers, promising to pay them "whatever is right" (Matt 20:4). At noon, he did the same thing, and again midafternoon; the harvest, it seems, was plentiful beyond his expectation. Finally, late in the afternoon, he went out to hire even more workers. When nightfall came, each of the workers was paid, beginning with those who had been hired for only an hour. These were given a full day's wage, in spite of the fact that they had only worked a brief time. Next came those who were hired midafternoon, and they received the same amount. And so it went until those who had worked the entire day were paid a full day's wage as they had agreed upon. But "when they had received it, they grumbled against the landowner, saying, 'These last worked only one hour, and you have made *them* equal to *us* who have borne the burden of the day and the scorching heat'" (20:11–12).

We might feel the same sense of injustice upon hearing the story as the full-day workers felt when their longer service was rewarded no more highly than the latecomers. Surely, the parable refers to objections raised by some Christians who have long been in the faith that *they* can expect no *higher* place of honor than the most wretched sinner who only *belatedly* repents and so is saved. But along the way, Jesus provides a startling lesson in the way God looks at economic matters. There was a very *humane reason* that someone who was hired for only an hour or two after standing around in the employment office for most of the day without a job was given the same payment of a denarius that the laborer who worked all day long was given: no one could support a family on anything less. And so, what was *right* was a full day's wage. In the way God reestablishes the world, enough is provided for all, nothing over, and no shortage. God is trusted, and God is faithful. To do otherwise is to run back to Egypt, to put our trust in *Pharaoh* and *Pharaoh's* storehouses and *Pharaoh's* calendar rather than to commit ourselves to *God* and to *God's* grace and to *God's* gracious *rhythm* of *life*.

I don't suppose that anyone here is happy about working ourselves to death—not just as individuals, but as a society. We know that God created us for more than that. One of the commentators I was reading this week reminded me about something I have seen in Mexico—how the peasants there, barely making enough to put food on the table, yet always have enough to buy some flowers to put on the table as well—a simple but eloquent testimony that, in fact, we really do *not* live by bread alone. "I will test them," God said, "whether they will follow my instruction or not" (Exod 16:4). But what can we do to witness to the rightness of *God's* economy in the face of what we are told are the realities of the *world's* economy? We still must choose which master we will serve. We at least can choose what we will buy—how the products are made and under what conditions, and what their long-term effect on us and our neighbors will be. We at least can choose to live more simply—giving up any competition for the status of wealth, or the false securities of money and things. We at least can acknowledge that solemn *rest* is as important in *God's* sight as *hard work*, and no market forces can justify disrupting the rhythm that *God* has ordained. We at least can testify in our board rooms and government halls that, in the world God created, there *is* enough for *all*, and all will *receive* enough when *God's* purposes guide human behavior. We at least can remember that God has promised faithfully to provide what we truly need, and rest content that the one who sacrificed on the cross what was most dear of all—Jesus Christ—to give us freedom from fear and anxiety, from sin and death, surely will not leave us to starve in some wilderness.

Twenty-sixth Sunday in Ordinary Time

Spanish Springs Presbyterian Church, Sparks, Nevada

September 25, 2005

Exodus 17:1–7
Philippians 2:1–13
Matthew 21:23–32

"God in Our Wilderness"

There's an old saying: A week is a lifetime in politics. George Romney, Edmund Muskie, and Howard Dean all learned the truth of that. When you are out in the public eye, and the press is supportive and the public is enchanted, nothing could be sweeter. But a miscalculated admission of having been "brainwashed," or an un-leader-like reply to a mean-spirited criticism of one's spouse, or an intemperate yelp caught on videotape, and it's all over. Even more quickly than in sports, being a public leader means that if you are *today's hero*, you can easily become *tomorrow's goat*, and vice versa.

As in so many other instances, the Bible is well aware of *this* truth, too. The greatest of all Old Testament heroes—still reckoned by Jews as the greatest of the prophets—was the first biblical character to be booed by the crowd. The man before whose staff the waters of the Red Sea had parted and allowed the Israelites to escape from their slavery, and then before whose staff the waters of the Red Sea crashed in again upon the pursuing army of Pharaoh—surely something to impress even the most hard-boiled newspaper reporter or draw a compliment from one's fiercest political opponent—within days afterward was in fear of being stoned to death by the very people he had rescued. Short attention spans are not unique to the current generation. Ingratitude is not a brand-new phenomenon. Public fickleness is not a modern development. And no generation or race has a monopoly on unfaith. So what happened?

Rather immediately after Moses had sung his song of praise and thanksgiving to God for delivering the Israelites from bondage, miraculously opening up the waters of the sea for the slaves and then releasing them back again on Pharaoh's horsemen and charioteers, the people had complained that they were thirsty (parents, you can imagine what that sounded like) and that the only water they could find was bad. Moses appealed to God, and God showed Moses a piece of wood, and Moses tossed it in the pool, and the water was made sweet, and then they came to an oasis. They kept on going along toward the promised land, and on the fifteenth day they complained that they were hungry (parents, you can imagine what *that* sounded like), and God responded by sending them quail in the evening and manna in the morning, and *continued* to do so throughout their journey. But as they left the wilderness of Sin and came to a place called Rephidim and camped there, there was no water. "The people quarreled with Moses, and said, 'Give us water to drink.' Moses said to them, 'Why do you quarrel with me? Why do you test the Lord?' But the people thirsted there for water; and the people complained against Moses and said, 'Why did you bring us out of Egypt, to kill us and our children and livestock with thirst?' So Moses cried out to the Lord, 'What shall I do with this people? They are almost ready to stone me'" (Exod 17:2–5).

Now, to be fair, it wasn't as if the people had a long history of relying upon God, or even *worshiping* God. They had no Bible. They had no temple or synagogues or holy places, all that long time in Egypt. There were no priests yet. They wouldn't even have had a *name* for God, not until Moses told them what had happened to him at the burning bush. They had some sense that they were a people, a race, the descendants of Abraham and Isaac and Jacob, but they did not yet know *whose* they were, or what that implied or might require of them. They didn't know that they were unique in God's estimation, and their circumstances of captivity wouldn't have suggested such a thing. They had only known the hardship and indignity of slavery, and had never had any experience of freedom, but, on the other hand, neither had they ever wanted of food or water; after all, it would have been pointless for the Egyptians to have slaves and not give them something to eat and something to drink. Having a dependable source of food and water seemed pretty good, no matter the cost, compared with chasing mirages across the desert all day long.

We sometimes hear of people who accuse others of not having enough faith. Cruelly, that implies that people's illnesses, people's oppression, people's poverty are really their own fault. And so, when a truly *faithful* person *does* get sick, *does* fall under oppression, *does* lose a job and can't find another one, and believes that it's because he or she isn't a good enough Christian, it genuinely becomes a crisis of faith. Countless preachers over the centuries have used this passage as an example of a people who didn't trust God, and as a warning to their congregations not to be faithless. Curiously, though, God doesn't seem to have been upset over the people's complaints—not nearly as exercised over them as Moses was. It was *Moses* who, afterward, called the place of the people's grumbling criticism "Massah and Meribah" (17:7), meaning "test" and "quarrel;" *God* doesn't seem to have told him to do so. It had more to do with *Moses'* injured pride and bruised sense of entitlement than any offense felt by *God*. And the fact is that God didn't give water or food the *first* time until the people *had* grumbled about it—there *was* no good water until God had shown Moses the piece of wood that he threw into the pool (who would have thought of *that*?), and there *were* no quail and there *was* no manna until the people complained that they were hungry, no Starbucks just around the next corner, no Denny's just over the horizon. So, if there was *any* crisis of faith here, it seems more to have been a crisis about *Moses'* faith than about the *Israelites'* faith. There's more of an immediate lesson here—if lesson there *be*—for *ministers* than for *congregations*. For *his* part, *God* did not panic, *God* did not become vindictive, *God* did not rant and rave about the people's lack of faith. God simply and rather matter-of-factly said to Moses, "'Go on ahead of the people, and take some of the elders of Israel with you; take in your hand the staff with which you struck the Nile, and go. I will be standing there in front of you on the rock at Horeb. Strike the rock, and water will come out of it, so that the people may drink.' Moses did so, in the sight of the elders of Israel" (17:5–6). Judging from the tone of the narrative, it was just another day at the office for God.

And yet, of course, it *wasn't*. This was the people whom God had selected for himself, the people for whom God had worked a great and powerful act of liberation at the cost of thousands of Egyptian lives, the people upon whom God pinned hopes for bringing all of creation back into a right relationship with God—the relationship for which God had created the world to begin with. Their welfare was of supreme importance to God. And so, when they moaned and groaned about hunger and thirst, God did not lecture them, God did not threaten them, God did not have second thoughts about having chosen them. God destined the people not for *slavery*, but for *freedom*. God didn't want the people he had saved from slavery to *return* to Egypt, but to forge ahead to the promised land of freedom and prosperity. So God *fed* them and gave them *water*, even water from a hard, dry, sun-baked rock. And, thus, the story tells us not so much about the *faithlessness* of the *people*, rather, more about the *fragile* faith of *Moses*, and a *whole lot* about the faithfulness of *God*.

"God in Our Wilderness"

The story of the Israelites' complaining of being thirsty and hungry and God giving them water and giving them food is not a story of *warning*, but a story of *assurance*. It was *Moses* who said that the people were testing God. If that were true—if the people *were* putting God to the test by complaining about lack of food and water when, in fact, there *was* no food and water until *after* they had complained and there *wouldn't* have been food or water if they *hadn't* complained—then God seems to have had no objection, but simply responded, not in a wimpishly indulgent way, but in an eminently practical way. The danger—the sin, if you will—would come in taking God's faithfulness for *granted* and becoming *ungrateful*, ungrateful even to the point of *disobeying* God, *disregarding* the law that God, just a few chapters later, commanded his people to obey as the way of showing their genuine gratitude for *having* food to eat and water to drink, for having been relieved of their oppression in Egypt and for being led to a land flowing with milk and honey which would be their very own. It seems to me perfectly natural for the Israelites to have said to Moses, "What now?" after finding themselves, at God's behest, wandering in the middle of an empty and waterless wilderness. But the miracle of liberation did not end with the parting of the Red Sea. God did not free them from Pharaoh just to leave them to starve and die of thirst.

Have you ever found yourself providentially removed from one bad situation just to find yourself then in a sort of wilderness of uncertainty, barren of prospects? *We* have, in *our* family, resigning a job for conscience' sake, and then being a little bewildered that another door did not fling open immediately, and so the belts tightened, and the bills mounted up. It is just what some people fear about leaving abusive and destructive marriages—escaping the abuse and dysfunction, all right, but maybe at the cost of finding oneself out on the street, cut off from family, forgotten by friends. In a hundred other different ways, we may find ourselves thinking that we are following God's gracious lead, going through doors that God has miraculously opened for us to escape this situation or that, and after the first few exhilarating moments of breathing the air of freedom, suddenly noticing that there is no oasis on the horizon. Freedom can be a frightening thing, even if it's what we truly believe God wants for us.

But the people of God who, over many centuries, wrote and preserved and cherished the book of Exodus, and the entire Bible, did so not simply to tell a story of what happened once upon a long time ago, but because the story has been verified and reaffirmed over and over again in human experience. What God did for the thirsty and hungry Israelites of old, God still does for thirsty and hungry people today. The God who freed slaves over three thousand years ago is at work liberating nations and races and societies and individuals in the year 2005, often through prophetic liberators not *un*like Moses. The God who responded to the people's quite reasonable need for water and food in the desert of Sinai responds *today* to the real needs of people in their barren wilderness of inner city, of suburbia, of rural farmland, wherever the dust is threatening to choke God's promise of abundant life. And the even greater wonder of God raising Jesus Christ from that ultimate symbol of despair, the grave, is the conclusive test of God's ability to work a miracle in a barren landscape—a test not imposed upon God by complaining humankind, but rather a test that God imposed upon himself, not to *quiet* human *grumbling* but to *soothe* human *tears*, and God's *own* tears shed for the creatures he loves, who are so often lost in deserts of their own making. No landscape is barren of hope, because God has shown himself faithful to be present in our wilderness, and to answer our cries with a spring of water that will never run dry, and food from heaven that will fill us and sustain us for the rocky journey into the promised land. And God *will* not, God *does* not, despise or disregard our very real *physical* needs on that journey through the wilderness any more than God despised or disregarded the very real physical needs of the Israelites—bread from heaven, perhaps by way of the Food Bank of Northern Nevada distributing to hungry people the very food that you brought to church two weeks ago on communion Sunday, or that you will bring next Sunday for World Communion Sunday; water from a rock, perhaps the pure bottled water for the victims of Hurricane Katrina purchased by your dollars given last spring through One Great Hour of Sharing or last week through the special Hurricane Katrina relief fund; or the word of comfort and hope you spoke a few days ago to a friend in despair, or the job referral you passed on to a neighbor desperately needing out of his or her current employment. That's why this story of God's faithful response to thirsty and hungry people is *in* the Bible—it gives us assurance of something that is vitally true even today. The God who cared enough about his people of old to free them from bondage didn't abandon them in the wilderness, but was present with them there and cared for them and provided for them all their journey *through* the wilderness to the land God had promised them. And God is present in *our* wilderness, too.

Twenty-seventh Sunday in Ordinary Time

Spanish Springs Presbyterian Church, Sparks, Nevada

October 2, 2011

Exodus 20:1–4, 7–9, 12–20
Philippians 3:4b–14
Matthew 21:33–46

"Taste, and See"

The word "flesh" appears many places in the Bible. Sometimes, it means the stuff that we're made of. Sometimes, it is a way of referring to all created beings. Sometimes, its meaning is not so tangible. Particularly in the writings of Paul, it is susceptible to misunderstanding. In today's culture, with its preoccupation with sex—and I mean both those who promote promiscuity and those who seem to think that it is the only *real* sin—a lot of people are inclined to read "lust" and "eroticism" into the word that Paul used so frequently in his letters, often speaking of "the flesh" in a negative way. But Paul used the word "flesh" in several other ways, too, many of them negative—and not simply as a reference to sexual appetite, unbridled and animalistic. More often, when he spoke critically about "the flesh," he was referring to that dimension of the human creature that is self-centered, eager to satisfy its own desires whatever they might be, supposing itself to be its own master, observing only its own laws of self-gratification, disregarding of the damage and injury it may do to others in the process. "The flesh" is really the person turned in on him- or herself, supposing him- or herself to be independent, autonomous, subject to no thing and to no one, and free to do whatever he or she wishes without regard to the effect on others or consequences to the environment.

Ironically, in this sense of the word, even people who adhere rigorously to the laws of God set forth in scripture can be more of "the flesh" than of "the spirit." Righteousness is a goal toward which all people should strive. Everyone should want, above anything else in their lives, to be in a proper relationship with God, who gives us life and sustains our life and invites us into life eternal, overflowing with love and peace. But obsession with righteousness as something that can be measured and compared to *other* people's goodness leads to *self*-righteousness, the belief that we can save ourselves, are even *responsible* for saving ourselves, which usually involves proving *our* righteousness by condemning *other* people whose faults we have detected. Paul himself had once been in that category—his training as a Pharisee sharpened his ability to scrutinize others, made his nose more sensitive to the whiff of moral deviation.

In our desire for a black-and-white world, we often think of Paul as having been woefully ignorant of God before his experience on the road to Damascus, his mind in shadows and his heart in an icebox, else how could he have persecuted the followers of Christ, standing by approvingly, for instance, when Stephen was stoned to death? The caption at the top of the page in my favorite Bible where Paul, then known as Saul, "still breathing threats and murder against the disciples of the Lord, went to the high priest and asked him for letters to the synagogues at Damascus, so that if he found any who belonged to the Way, men or women, he might bring them bound to Jerusalem" (Acts 9:1–2), but then, "as he was going along and approaching Damascus, suddenly a light from heaven flashed all around him" (9:3) and "he fell to the ground and heard a voice saying to him, 'Saul, Saul, why do you persecute me?'" (9:4) and he asked, "Who are you, Lord?" (9:5a) and the voice answered, "I am Jesus, whom you are persecuting" (9:5b), and he lost his eyesight, but then something like scales fell from his eyes and he was baptized, refers to the episode as "The Conversion of Saul."[1] But that begs the question. Converted to *what*? Converted *from* what? There was no separate set of doctrine or even rules known as "Christianity." If he was on his way to Damascus to scour the synagogues there, what he would have found were *Jews*—but Jews who, unlike him, no longer looked to the *law* as the source of their righteousness and the guarantee of their salvation, but to *Jesus Christ*.

Years after that experience, Paul, in a letter to the members of the church at Philippi in Macedonia, explained how, as a Pharisee, he had trusted in his ability to obey perfectly the Ten Commandments and all the other laws of scripture. He called it "confidence in the flesh" (Phil 3:4)—confidence, in other words, in his independence and autonomy and self-sufficiency. Oh, he wouldn't have thought that that was where his confidence was in the days

---

1. *New Oxford Annotated Bible: New Revised Standard Version*, 173 NT.

before he had set out to Damascus. If anyone had asked Saul where his faith lay, he would undoubtedly have said, "In God." And he would have meant it, and been shocked that anyone could think otherwise. But in the days and months and years since he had come to know and appreciate and love the one who had been condemned according to the law and who had been put to death according to the law and who had been buried according to the law but then had appeared to him along the road as he was busily and officiously carrying out his self-appointed task of keeping Judaism pure, Paul had come to discover what God, and life as a child of the covenant, were really all about. And he must have been very surprised indeed at first to learn that it was *not* about winning a trophy for *keeping* all of the *laws* better than anyone else.

But before any of us jumps to the conclusion that that means the law is unimportant and we can ignore it all, we need to acknowledge that Paul did not denounce his former life, did not belittle those who strive for moral perfection, did not turn his back on his Jewish heritage. He simply came to recognize that that was not the same thing as *faith* in God. He still identified himself as having been circumcised just as the law said it should happen, was as blue-blooded as any Jew could possibly be, devoted to the commandments and the statutes and the regulations, zealous even, legally impeccable as far as human judgment could determine. And that was quite an achievement. But he now knew it to be largely *irrelevant*, that *fleshly* way of assessing one's worth, because it had all really boiled down to having faith not in *God*, but in *himself*.

Having faith in *God* required a generous space for *grace*—God's *mercy*, God's *love* even for the *undeserving*, God's zeal to bring into the gates of his kingdom even the most *wayward* person, which, Paul came to recognize, meant perhaps the most legally-observant but also the most self-congratulatory person he knew—*himself*. "Whatever gains I had, these I have come to regard as loss because of Christ" (3:7). Paul wasn't walking *away from* or even *repenting of* his Jewishness, or his observance of the law. But none of those things, good and useful and important as they were, was Christ Jesus, the perfect expression of God's love and goal for all humankind born, crucified, and raised from the tomb in flesh, now alive and powerful in spirit, and who, for everyone who has faith in him, is life itself which cannot be taken away by the sufferings of this world but binds us to God for all eternity. So, Paul said, "whatever gains I had, these I have come to regard as loss because of Christ. More than that, I regard everything as loss because of the surpassing value of knowing Christ Jesus my Lord. For his sake I have suffered the loss of all things, and I regard them as rubbish, in order that I may gain Christ and be found in him, not having a righteousness of my own that comes from the law, but one that comes through faith in Christ, the righteousness from God based on faith" (3:7–9).

Paul had been raised to new life, free of the fleshly qualities of jealousy and pride and fear and greed and, yes, lust, by his belief in the resurrection of Christ. Righteousness was no longer about *him*, but about *Christ*. He no longer imagined that he could manufacture his *own* goodness—whatever goodness there *was* in him was something that was imputed *to* him from *Christ*. As Martin Luther expressed it, reflecting on Paul's writings, when God looks at someone who has faith in Christ, God sees *Christ*, and *his* perfect righteousness.[2] But if we share in Christ's *resurrection*, Paul reminded his readers, we also share in his *sufferings*. And that, of course, is something that, intuitively, we would rather not do. The flesh—the weakness of our human nature, even in all its best values and achievements—argues against it, is inclined to reject Christ, to put him out of its way, as happened so cruelly and completely at Calvary. The flesh asserts its true nature by opposing any suggestion that it may have to die with Christ, to suffer in any way, to give up any of its own desires and discard its own earthly measures of success. The flesh balks at any notion of sacrificing itself. That, of course, makes it impossible to be raised with Christ.

What we observe today on this World Communion Sunday as, with Christians everywhere, we come to the table of grace and reconciliation, is the willingness with which Christ gave himself up on the cross for the salvation of the world, surrendering not only his *flesh*, represented in the bread broken and the wine poured, but all fleshly *desire*, all fleshly *pride*, all fleshly *ambition*, all fleshly notion of *success*. From a *fleshly* point of view, Jesus was a complete *failure*. From a *fleshly* point of view, therefore, we would be *fools* to *follow* him. But when God overturned all human judgment and fleshly appearance by raising Jesus from the grave, God showed in the most unequivocal way, to people who have eyes to see, that Jesus was, is, in fact, the Son of God, beloved and approved, the very expression of everything that God values in creation and everything that God hopes for in humankind. So Paul finally "*saw*," when something like scales fell from his eyes—the blinders, perhaps, of pride, of judgmentalism, of self-righteousness, of "the flesh."

That is really what this meal is all about. Remembering the selfless love, the humble service, the sacrificial death, of the one and only person entitled to all honor and glory and power but who surrendered it completely, willingly and obediently, in total trust of God's will and purpose and eternal love, we come to this table in witness that not a single one of us is deserving of even a *crumb*, even a *drop*—that none of us has done anything to earn a

---

2. J. Alton Templin, Iliff School of Theology, winter term, 1978.

place at this meal, or to earn our salvation, no matter how well we keep the law, no matter how neat our lawns or how well-behaved our children, no matter how perfect our marriages or how prestigious our jobs—not that those things aren't good and to be highly commended. But none of that makes us acceptable to God or entitles us to God's generous care, including our daily bread. Only God's gracious love, undeserved, demonstrated at unimaginable cost, coursing through the world today in the faithful words and deeds of those who measure the value of their own lives not by what *they* have *done* but by what *God* has been willing to do *for* them—sacrifice even his own Son because even the least of us, wretched, sinful, self-consumed, is that precious to him. Come, taste, and see.

Twenty-eighth Sunday in Ordinary Time

First Presbyterian Church, Ponca City, Oklahoma

October 19, 2014

Exodus 32:1–14
Philippians 1:4–9
Matthew 22:1–14

"God on Our Terms?"

The Bible is the unique and authoritative written witness to God's will. But it is not only that. The Bible is also the greatest literary achievement in history. One of the things that is so striking about the Bible as literature is its fine use of the literary device of irony. And nowhere in the Bible is the irony so great as between *last* Sunday's reading from Exodus and *this* Sunday's reading from Exodus.

Last week, we read of Moses the great prophet on Mount Sinai receiving God's explicit instructions about how the people he had led up out of slavery must live in freedom. "I am the Lord your God, who brought you out of the land of Egypt, out of the house of slavery; you shall have no other gods before me. You shall not make for yourself an idol, whether in the form of anything that is in heaven above, or that is on the earth beneath, or that is in the water under the earth. You shall not bow down to them or worship them; for I the Lord your God am a jealous God" (Exod 20:2–5a). *This* Sunday we read:

> When the people saw that Moses delayed to come down from the mountain, the people gathered around Aaron, and said to him, "Come, make gods for us, who shall go before us; as for this Moses, the man who brought us up out of the land of Egypt, we do not know what has become of him." Aaron said to them, "Take off the gold rings that are on the ears of your wives, your

> sons, and your daughters, and bring them to me." . . . He took the gold from them, formed it in a mold, and cast an image of a calf; and they said, "These are your gods, O Israel, who brought you up out of the land of Egypt!" (32:1–2, 4)

Did you hear that? At the very moment that Moses was high up on the mountaintop receiving God's commandment to have no other gods, and to make for themselves no idols, the people were down in the valley fashioning a metal statue to worship, a golden calf molded from their own jewelry that Pharaoh had given them and they brought with them from Egypt. The people had just walked miraculously through the Red Sea on dry land. The people had just miraculously received manna in the morning and quails in the evening. The people had seen Moses beat a rock with his staff and watched as water miraculously gushed forth. These wonders did not just happen by themselves. God had responded faithfully to the people's every need. But already, now, they were turning away from God in rebellion and idolatry. Already they violated the most important and fundamental of the commandments.

God was too slow. God was too remote. God was too uncontrollable. They decided to do something about it. They would have a god whom they could carry and set down, a god they could see and touch, a god they could put in a box when they were tired of worshiping him. They would have God on *their* terms. And Israel fell with its first step. The people of God were faithful not much longer than Adam and Eve had been, back in the garden in Genesis. God was chagrined and insulted; the very people that he had chosen for his own, had saved from the misery of bondage in Egypt, had provided water and bread for in the wilderness, turned away from the living and powerful and liberating God to a statue—an image of an ox that eats grass. And God told Moses to leave him alone, that he might destroy them in his anger. Indeed, only the intercession of Moses, who refused to stand aside in the matter, seems to have saved the people from the punishment they deserved. And after Moses reasoned with God for a while ("What about your promise? Think of what the neighbors will say!")—only after that, God changed his mind about abandoning the people to their fate, as if a statue had any power to save!

It is tempting for us to dismiss as irreligious, even wicked, the Israelites who turned to worship the golden calf. But scripture gives us no reason to believe that they were particularly bad people. Their experience with matters of faith was still quite new. For generations, they had been surrounded by statues of gods in Egypt. Far from being *ir*religious, the incident with the golden calf shows that they were just the opposite—they were *very* religious.

The need to have the divine in their midst was foremost in their minds. They wanted something to bow down to. Their hunger for the *divine* was even *greater* than their love of *gold*—they sacrificed their riches just so they could have a god they could *see*.

And yet, of course, the golden calf was *not* God. It was a product of their own invention, a thing, a device, something to suit *their* notion of what a god should be like, a god who can be brought out and a god who can be put away, a god who could perhaps even be melted down again if things didn't work out the way Israel wanted them to, a god scaled to human standards, a god fashioned by human hands. They wanted to control their god. They wanted to define the nature and way of God according to their own desires. The fact that the psalmist remembered the story, the fact that Isaiah remembered the story, shows that the folly of the golden calf weighed on the conscience of Israel throughout its history. It suggests, as well, that idolatry remained an ever-present danger throughout Israel's history. Constantly, the people of Israel needed to be reminded of how they had once tried to cast God in their own mold, to their own specifications, and how that was not only silly, but very nearly deadly.

"Oh, those ignorant people!" we think. But, you know, Christians are not immune to such mistakes. Our very religious nature sometimes tempts *us* to seek a tangible substitute for the *in*visible God. Our very zeal for spiritual truth may sometimes prompt us to mold God to the contours of our own preferences—the result being that we strip God of the very freedom and sovereignty that define who God is, so that we worship not a God of liberating power, but a God of paralyzing bondage.

What is *tragic* for *individuals* becomes *fatal* to the *church*. When we substitute our personal ideas about God for God's own revelation—when we work ourselves into a frenzy of religious invention in the *valley* while God is patiently spelling out the means to righteousness on the *mountaintop*—we are repeating the folly of the golden calf, invariably trying to fashion God according to the cultural deities of our time—what is popular, what is entertaining, what suits human inclination, what is convenient, what is easy. Then we wheel out a god who has our prejudices, our suspicions, even our hatreds—a god who matches our agenda and fits our schedule, a cut-and-paste job that borrows a little bit from scripture and a little bit from economics and a little bit from commercial music and a little bit from advice columns and, lately, a whole lot from politics.

It is in order to avoid creating a god according to our personal tastes and opinions that each member of this and every church should be actively engaged in serious regular study about the faith with other Christians. I say that as the person specially charged with your spiritual health. Our classes here, including our adult classes, should be bulging, not because the curriculum is fun or the teacher is witty, but because we need to know what God *wants* of us, and what God wants of us *today*. We can hardly expect the *children* entrusted to our care to develop that discipline if our *adults* do not model it. The Christian church must not deny, and no part of it can afford to ignore, that God very nearly gave up on a people who decided that they would have God on their *own* terms, popular and convenient and selective.

The chief priests and scribes and Pharisees thought that *they* knew all *about* God, and so they had Jesus arrested and crucified. In fact, even though they had the *scriptures*—the law and the prophets—they had managed to create a god according to their *own* notions of what was right and wise and practical and holy. Theirs was a god of rigidity, a god of exclusion, a god not much interested in the world that *they* taught he had created. Then *Jesus* came along, forgiving the very people *they* labeled as vile sinners, breaking the law and showing contempt for good order and defying principles of financial administration by gathering grain on the sabbath, healing on the sabbath, driving out the money changers and profiteers from the temple, befriending folk the Pharisees and chief priests and scribes considered to be untouchable, and including in his own inner circle even people of ill repute. The Pharisees and chief priests and scribes were not *bad*; they were some of the most respected folk in the Jewish community—the pillars of Jewish society, who never would have considered committing adultery or murder or theft or idolatry—not overtly, anyway. But they had molded an image of God according to their own standards—standards that sounded holy enough, seemed pious enough, looked plausible enough, but which substituted their *own* judgments about the divine for the truth of the inner heart of God.

Jesus told a parable that Matthew reported as an allegory—a story about a king who hosted a marriage feast for his son. He had invited a number of people—undoubtedly all the nobility and the social list of the kingdom. When he sent out his servants to announce to the invited guests that the joyful activity had begun, that their places at the table were ready, some of the guests—farmers and business types, busy people—decided that they had more important things to do—their work, being productive. The king's invitation proved to be inconvenient for them, apparently, so they didn't come to the king's table. Others, offended somehow by the king's servants, treated them nastily and eventually destroyed them. What they heard didn't suit them, so they did away with the messengers. So "the king was enraged. He sent his troops, destroyed those murderers, and burned their city. Then he said to his slaves, 'The wedding is ready, but those invited were not worthy. Go therefore into the main streets, and invite everyone you find to the wedding banquet.' Those slaves went out into the streets and gathered all whom they found, both good and bad; so the wedding hall was filled with guests" (Matt 22:7–10).

The banquet table must have looked very different from what those who had originally been invited to the feast, but chose not to respond, would have expected—beggars, vagabonds, the unwashed and the unmannered, the sick, the blind, the lame, the leper, the tax collector, the prostitute. If the *original* guests had walked into the banquet hall and found such people there, they surely would have stomped right back out again. Who in their right mind would think that a king would want *these* at his table? It hardly fits *our* image of a king. Does it fit our image of *God*?

The Israelites stumbled badly when, in their religious zeal, they chose to have a god on their *own* terms, conforming to their *own* notions, instantly available to drag out or push aside, as they desired. God very nearly abandoned them to start over again with a *new* chosen people. Jesus made it clear in parable that God is *still* capable of looking *elsewhere* if *Christians* or any *group* of Christians decide that it is too inconvenient to answer God's invitation to join in the festivities at his table—that there are more *important* things to be doing, or *easier* things, or more *amusing* things. In our smorgasbord society, we mustn't confuse the king of creation with Burger King—nowhere in the Bible does it say, "Have it *your* way." If *we* choose the terms on which God will be *with* us, God will *call* us, God will *command* us, God will *expect* something of us, then *we* have created a golden calf. God on *our* terms is not God at *all*.

The terms on which God comes to us are the life, death, and resurrection of Jesus Christ, who told us to love God with all our heart, and love our neighbor as ourself; who commissioned us to be servants; who commanded us to forgive freely; who directed us to show hospitality generously; who taught us to despise no one; who instructed us to seek out each *other's* company and to seek out the *lost*; who wants us to be so trusting of God's care that we surrender everything we have to God's use. Do we really want God on *our* terms?—a god of our prejudices, a god of our appetites, a god of our culture, a god of our convenience? What a poor substitute that would be for the God who gave us Jesus Christ.

Twenty-ninth Sunday in Ordinary Time

First Presbyterian Church, Norfolk, Nebraska

October 21, 1990

Exodus 33:12–23
1 Thessalonians 1:1–10
Matthew 22:15–22

"When Faith Comes Alive"

"We always give thanks to God for all of you" (1 Thess 1:2a). How those words must have thrilled the Thessalonian Christians, coming as they did from Paul the apostle of the Lord, the preacher and teacher of the gospel of Jesus Christ, the missionary who with Silas and Timothy had founded the church at Thessalonica in Greece, perhaps the first Christian congregation in Europe! "We always give thanks to God for all of you and mention you in our prayers" (1:2). What encouraging tidings for a people who had been so tormented by persecutors, even as Paul himself had been abused by opponents and, more to the point, even as their Lord Jesus Christ had suffered at the hands of those who wanted to silence the truth of God! "We always give thanks to God for all of you and mention you in our prayers, constantly remembering before our God and Father your work of faith" (1:2–3a). What a marvelous affirmation for brand-new disciples whose first bold steps in the faith seemed perhaps so feeble in comparison with the great need to proclaim the gospel to the four corners of the world and to demonstrate the lordship of Christ Jesus in every aspect of life—private and public, personal and social!

"We always give thanks to God for all of you and mention you in our prayers, constantly remembering before our God and Father your work of faith and labor of love and steadfastness of hope in our Lord Jesus Christ. For we know, brothers and sisters beloved by God, that he has chosen you" (1:2-4). Imagine God choosing *them*—not children of Abraham, but Gentiles, people of no great importance by human standards, but ordinary folk with ordinary problems and ordinary abilities, some of whom had occasionally come to the door of the Jewish synagogue to listen and who observed Jewish laws in some degree, but who had never before heard the gracious words that God's promise was broad enough to include them! Imagine Christ having died for *them*—*sinners*, idolaters even, people who had probably never before heard of a mercy so complete that it could forgive any injury or wrongdoing, love so deep that it could move a person to give up life itself in order to save another! Imagine the Holy Spirit coming among *them* in power—working such transformations among them, turning them away from their accustomed selfish pleasures to endure suffering without complaint for the sake of the gospel, infusing such vibrant faith into their hearts that it was considered remarkable by all who heard of it!

The Thessalonian church is one of the true success stories in the spread of the gospel during the missionary career of Paul. If any congregation would have been justified in adopting a cautious approach to Christianity, it would have been *these* new believers. If any people would have had reason to doubt the wisdom of becoming disciples of the risen Lord, it would have been *these*. Nowhere was the resistance to the gospel and the persecution of Christians greater than in Thessalonica—according to the book of Acts, the Jews in that place fomented an uprising against Paul and Silas and attacked some of the new believers. The apostles had to escape to a nearby town. When the mob from Thessalonica pursued them even there, Paul had to escape again, going eventually to Athens. Now, sometime later, Paul has received word from Timothy of the faith and love of these new Christians. Paul writes to answer some questions and to express his great thanksgiving, mindful of this church's "work of faith and labor of love and steadfastness of hope in our Lord Jesus Christ" (1:3b).

Each time I read First Thessalonians, I am struck by the note of zestful Christianity which leaps from the page. Paul and his associates seem not to be giving a pep talk to a group of tired Christians, Christians for whom the faith has become something familiar and customary and comfortable, for whom the fires of conviction have become only warm embers and for whom Christianity has lost the thrill of adventure. The Thessalonian Christians were believers aflame with the love of Christ, genuinely excited about their faith and the things that the Holy Spirit was doing within their congregation and their individual lives, so sure of the truth of the gospel that they were willingly hazarding both their lives and their fortunes. They had turned their backs on the false gods of their culture to serve the living Lord with a passion and fervor so remarkable that their moral uprightness, their spiritual activity, their constancy in spite of trial and affliction were being talked about throughout the Christian world. Not that it was all or even primarily their *own* doing—the Christian virtues of faith, hope, and love had come to a living expression in the Thessalonians because God had made these people his very own and had breathed the Holy Spirit into their life together.

The life-transforming potential of the gospel of Jesus Christ has been attested not only in scripture, but within the actual experience of most of us. When I was in high school, a certain chap named Tim seemed always to be doing the most obnoxious things and making the most unkind remarks. He was smart, but insensitive. He seemed to delight in entertaining himself by causing others pain through sneer or embarrassment. His behavior was not simply a peculiarity of personality—it was genuine meanness. I admit that I did not like Tim. I could see no good ever coming from him. Perhaps as a youth, you had such an acquaintance in school; perhaps in your adulthood you have had such acquaintances at work, in social organizations, even in the church. At my tenth high school reunion—now more than eleven years ago—I don't suppose that there was anyone I less expected to see than Tim. In youth, he had seemed so thoughtless toward others that I would not have imagined his having any interest in renewing acquaintances. I recognized him immediately at the class picnic; unlike many of my classmates, he had changed hardly at all in appearance. But I doubt that any other of my classmates could possibly have changed so *completely* in *attitude*. As we shook hands, we exchanged the usual reunion pleasantries, including the obligatory "So what are *you* doing now?" And when I told Tim that I was enrolled in seminary part time, his face lit up like an electric sign. "Bruce," he said, "I have finally become a Christian, and the Lord has made such a difference in my life." Indeed, the Lord *had* made a difference in his life. As we grow from youth to adulthood, most of us mature in our behavior, but character traits that we have developed by the time we graduate from high school are usually well enough ingrained that they have at least a residual effect on our adult personality. But it quickly became apparent that Tim was a completely different person; so totally absent from him was any trace of the old insensitivity and arrogance that my heart sang for joy. Indeed, tears came to my eyes when Tim said, "I'm sorry for the way that I used to treat people."

Suddenly, it became clear to me that the Tim I had known ten years before had been a young man tragically at war with himself; the Tim who now stood before me had permitted himself to discover the peace of Jesus Christ—a peace which filled him to the brim and now flowed over into his relationships with all of those around him. He had joy in his own life, and the joy radiated out to the people around him. The old Tim no longer existed.

He had become a brand-new person. Jesus Christ had become incarnate in him, speaking with a warmth and tenderness of which I had supposed Tim to be totally incapable. I am quite certain that Tim would not mind my sharing this story with you—his only embarrassment would be that I might seem to be holding him up as any sort of model of faith. We had a beautiful conversation, free from all of the tensions that had formerly characterized everyone's dealings with him. And as we parted, I remember Tim's smile—a smile that I had never seen on his face in three years of high school, and I felt a little ashamed that I had ever disliked him, and more ashamed that my own progress in the faith seemed minuscule compared to his monumental journey, and even more ashamed that I had ever underestimated the boundless power of the Holy Spirit.

Paul saw such radical transformations everywhere he went. People were coming alive to new possibilities of love and forgiveness and courage and confidence and commitment. Having heard the good news, nothing mattered to them so much as loyalty to this God who came into the world in the person Jesus who died for them and was raised from the dead and now lives with God in power. No longer were the customary attitudes and the conventional behavior around them their standard. No longer were their imaginations of what *could* be and their expectations of what *would* be limited by what already *was* and what *had* been in the *past*. No longer was their horizon of concern limited to their selfish appetites and the welfare of their own little household. The good news of Jesus Christ had burst their cocoon of self-interest and set free a new creation, a new creation so marvelous that it amazed everyone around them and was remarked upon for hundreds of miles. "What about those Thessalonians?" people were asking. "What has gotten into them that has changed their lives so much, that has produced in them such works of faith and labors of love and steadfastness of hope?" The Thessalonian church was an example for which Paul could constantly give thanks.

Having heard of this Christian congregation almost two thousand years ago and half a world away, it is natural that we should ponder whether anyone has been prompted to ask such questions about *us*. Have we yet discovered the *excitement* of the Christian faith, the *adventure* of the Christian faith, the *danger* of the Christian faith, the *joy* of the Christian faith? How many of us does the good news of Jesus Christ inspire to the point that we are willing to step out of our comfortable routine, willing to risk letting go of the old securities, willing to surrender all lesser allegiances, willing to abandon even our old feuds and our un-Christlike prejudices? How many people in our own community or many miles away are marveling at our work of faith and labor of love and steadfastness of hope? At our whole-hearted participation in the worship of God and our eagerness to join with each other in study about the faith? At the way we encourage one another in faithfulness and celebrate each other's joys and comfort each other's sorrow? At our generosity in giving and our refusal to let differences become divisions? Do we share the excitement of those Christians for whom Paul gave his constant and joyful thanks—people for whom the faith was a life-transforming commitment, people who suffered every persecution and affliction for the sake of Christ, people who were aflame with their love of God in Jesus Christ and their love for God's creation? Do our words and actions and loyalties radiate the joy of the good news? Do our friends and family and acquaintances know that we are *excited* about the faith? There can be no greater joy, no greater excitement, than to have a living faith in Jesus Christ!

Thirtieth Sunday in Ordinary Time
First Presbyterian Church, Dodge City, Kansas
October 27, 1996

Deuteronomy 34:1–12
1 Thessalonians 2:1–8
Matthew 22:34–42

"Hold Nothing Back"

Bill and Mary Jones had completed the new member class just the week before. Now, as they prepared to go to worship and be publicly received into the membership of Middle Road Presbyterian Church, Mary remembered about the pledge card. It was the final ritual act of the membership class—being handed a pledge card by the moderator of the stewardship committee who had come, at the pastor's invitation, to say a few things about the financial needs of the church. She had spoken about pledging as an important discipline of putting Christ at the head of the household budget. She had talked about how a pledge is not a contract, but a good-faith indication of what a person intends to give, and how the amount can be adjusted down or up as circumstances change. She had taught how the pledge should really represent not only *money*, but time and abilities and prayers offered to Jesus Christ through his church, as well. She had shared how she and her family had discovered a curious thing when they decided to start striving to *tithe* to the church—to adopt a *goal* of giving the biblical standard of 10 percent of their income and to devote a proportionate amount of time and energy to the work of the congregation: they had discovered that they could not out-give the Lord. Every time they stretched themselves to give a little more, they found that they *had* that little more *available* to give.

Bill and Mary had heard such presentations before; they had moved around the country quite a bit, and had been members of several different churches. They hadn't meant to put off discussing their pledge amount, now that they were joining the congregation, but somehow it had gotten neglected during the week since the final session of the new member class. "Well," said Bill, "it's always a good idea to hold back a little, so that we can be in a position to increase it over the years. Plus, we don't know exactly what our living expenses will be in a new town. The mortgage payment is more than we've had before. We'll have to join the club to have a place to eat. And then there's the cost of school uniforms—the kids have never had those before. Put down ten dollars a week."

"But Bill," Mary reminded him, "that's where we started at our last church, and the church before that, several years ago. And we never *got around* to raising it. Our income is higher now, and the church can't make it today on yesterday's income any more than *we* could. Besides, that amount for our whole family *together* is not even the average amount given per *person* in the Presbyterian Church—I read that in *Presbyterians Today*."

"Still," Bill said, "we don't know how much we're going to have left here at the end of the month. We have to be conservative. We're not millionaires. We need to be prudent."

"OK," said Mary, "ten dollars a week it is," and she wrote the amount down on the card.

"How about getting away next weekend?" Bill asked, "—just the two of us? We need a break from all of this moving in."

"Can we afford it?" Mary asked.

"We'll manage," said Bill.

The Jones family was ushered to a vacant space near the front of the sanctuary, just in time to hear the announcements about the next weekend's Saturday workday at the church and the Sunday evening meeting for people who were interested in helping out with the youth program. The call to worship was issued, the hymn of praise was sung, the confession of sin and prayer for pardon was spoken, the assurance of pardon was declared, the scripture lessons were recited, the anthem was presented, and the sermon began. "You shall love the Lord your God with all your heart, and with all your soul, and with all your mind" (Matt 22:37 RSV), said the preacher.

The Pharisees and the scribes had been after Jesus. Jesus had been responding to them with parables—stories which challenged the comfortable assumption that their salvation was assured, and that those whom *they* excluded from *their* company, *God* would exclude from the *kingdom*. Then the Pharisees and Sadducees tried to trick Jesus into some misstatements about theology, but he foiled their attempts. Ultimately, one of the Pharisees, a man specially trained in the law of Moses, tested Jesus with a question: "Teacher, which is the great commandment in the law?" (22:36 RSV). Now, we have to remember that in Jesus' time, there were thought to be 613 separate commandments in the Bible—365 negative commandments, the same as the number of days in a year, and 248 positive commandments, the same as the number of parts in the body. Some people had managed to memorize them all. A few even managed to *observe* them all. But naturally, with so many separate laws, some of them came into conflict in particular cases. Most people could not expect and could not be expected to keep all of the many specific laws, so various teachers tried now and then to combine them or identify *some* as being more important than *others*. What the lawyer here was asking Jesus to do, others had attempted. Yet, anyone who would hazard to elevate one law over another was opening him- or herself to accusations of heresy and charges of being unfaithful. Most people realized, as we do today, officially, at least, that there is no hierarchy of sins, and, when it comes to serving the Lord, there can be no ranking of obligations.

Jesus answered shrewdly, but Jesus also answered truthfully. "You shall love the Lord your God with all your heart, and with all your soul, and with all your mind"—Deuteronomy chapter 6, verse 5. "This is the great and first commandment. And a second is like it, You shall love your neighbor as yourself"—Leviticus chapter 19, verse 18. "On these two commandments," Jesus said, "depend all the law and the prophets" (22:37–40 RSV). Bill and Mary Jones and the rest of us could smile with self-satisfaction at Jesus' response. *We* do that, we think—*we* love the Lord our God with heart, soul, and mind, and we even love our neighbor. *We* believe in God, especially the grandfatherly one. As for our neighbors, we may not *like* some of them much, but we manage to make room for them in the universe. Love of God and love for our fellows, after all, doesn't cost us anything. "You shall love the Lord your God with all your heart, and with all your soul, and with all your mind.... You shall love your neighbor as yourself" (22:37, 39 RSV).

The Bible's favorite word for "love"—the Greek word "agape"—means, in this context, the outpouring of one's whole being in devotion to another—giving oneself *completely* to *God*, giving oneself *completely* to a *neighbor*, and we cannot do *either* of those things without doing the *other*. We cannot love God in the sense that the *scriptures* mean "love" without loving our *neighbor*, and we cannot love our *neighbor* in the sense that the scriptures mean "love" without loving *God*. The one would simply die without the other, or prove to have no substance. And in both of those cases, the meaning is that we put ourselves and all that we have at the other's disposal. The word that the Bible uses here for "love" does not mean a *sentiment*, it means *action*. It is not *affection*, it is *commitment*. It does not stop at *warm feelings*, it is a *giving of oneself*. And yes, it *does* cost something. It requires *more* than just good intentions and nice thoughts. It requires *deeds*—sacrificial acts, costly acts. It requires a concrete commitment. It consists of doing good for the one who is loved, something tangible. And it requires that all of this be done *not* in a spirit of calculating the *least* that we can give, but striving to give the *most* that we can of ourselves and our resources for the benefit of the other, for the benefit of God and of neighbor, holding nothing back.

The Pharisees, and probably the lawyer who asked the question of Jesus in this episode, had been schooled to believe that a right relationship with God is a matter of keeping rules. Oh, they would surely make *offerings* to God—sacrifices in the temple, coins in the treasury. And, as they interpreted it, they were devoting their entire lives to God by studying the commandments and warning others not to break them. But, of course, they concentrated so much on rules like not exerting oneself on the sabbath and staying ritually clean that they actually *broke* the great commandment about loving their *neighbor*—doing their neighbor *good*. And in doing so, they automatically broke the great commandment about loving *God*. By *calculating* their righteousness, they never got to the point of loving God with all their heart and with all their soul and with all their mind. Not through legalistically checking off the list of commandments, but by observing the principle of loving God and loving neighbor without reserve, without limit, without calculation, without resentment, without *delay*, do we fulfill what God requires of us—giving ourselves fully in faith, trusting God so completely that we hold nothing back from God and hold nothing back from any neighbor for whom we can do good. And God has certainly gifted us generously today with everything we need to express our love of God and others through Christ's church. With all our heart, with all our soul, with all our mind—how can any of us ever approach giving to God in a spirit of begrudging, in a habit of calculating, in an attitude of how little we can "get by with"?

The minister finished the sermon, "Jesus said, 'You shall love the Lord your God with all your heart, and with all your soul, and with all your mind' (22:37 RSV). And 'You shall love your neighbor as yourself' (22:39 RSV). Jesus was saying, 'Hold nothing back.'"

Mary Jones noticed that her husband had been fidgeting in the pew for a while. At the end of the sermon, he leaned over and whispered, "Let me have the pledge card a minute." Mary fished it out of her purse and handed it to Bill. He scratched out the amount that she had written and put in a higher amount. "That's about what a weekend away would cost us," he whispered again as he handed the card back to her. She looked surprised, but pleased. "Well," he whispered in explanation, "there's that church workday next Saturday."

"And I would really like to learn about being a youth group sponsor," Mary answered. Then she added, "Bill, a weekend away from unpacking would have been nice, but I think we need to concentrate on living in our new home," and she pointed with a little sweep of her hand to the congregation seated all around them.

Thirty-first Sunday in Ordinary Time
Spanish Springs Presbyterian Church, Sparks, Nevada
October 31, 1999

Joshua 3:7–17
1 Thessalonians 2:9–13
Matthew 23:1–12

"What Is a Saint?"

As just about everyone knows, today is Halloween. The stores have been filled with candy and costumes for several weeks now. I was listening to a radio program in the car the other day that, if I heard correctly, claimed that Halloween is the second-biggest holiday, in terms of retail sales—in other words, right behind Christmas. One woman who was interviewed on the program explained that she likes Halloween so much because it is the only holiday on which it is impossible to go wrong—you don't have to worry about a meal turning out perfectly, or buying someone the right size sweater, or getting cards mailed on time. It was sort of strange, hearing *Halloween* compared with *Christmas*, but then I noticed the number of houses in our neighborhood that are decorated for the day—little plastic pumpkins and ghosts and witches hung in trees like you would hang ornaments on a Christmas tree, little ghost and pumpkin lights outlining the eaves of some houses, artificial cobwebs and tombstones and spiders and black cats, and the list goes on and on.

That got me thinking about the great distance between what has become the second-biggest retail event on the calendar and the *Christian* origin of the name "Halloween," which is a shortened form of "All Hallows' Eve," or the day and night immediately before All Saints' Day, November 1. The activities that we properly associate with Halloween are apparently traceable to the Druids, the ancient pagan worshipers who lived in parts of

Gaul and the British Isles about the time of Christ. It seems they believed that, on one night of the year, the lord of the dead called forth hosts of evil spirits. The Druids customarily lit great fires on Halloween in order to ward off all these spirits who were intent on revisiting their earthly homes on that night and frightening living human beings in the process. Somehow, that *pagan* belief about the return of the dead got connected with the *Christian* practice of celebrating all the Christian saints known and unknown. Originally, the Christian celebration of All Saints' Day took place in different places on different days of the year, but, in the 700s, it came to be fixed on November 1 in the Latin-speaking church. It's unfortunate that a non-Christian orgy of fright came to supplant the celebration of Christian sainthood in our culture, but perhaps that creates for ministers what we like to call a "teachable moment"—in this case, an opportunity for us to look at the question "What is a saint?"

In my library, I have a book titled *Dictionary of Saints*. It's a thick book, with articles on about five thousand individuals who, at one time or another in the history of the church, have been officially or popularly reckoned "saints." The introduction to the book explains,

> The saints are a fascinating company of men, women, and children who devoted their lives to Christ and his teachings in widely varied ways. They came from every walk of life—from poor peasant tilling his soil to eke out a living and poverty-stricken slum dweller of a large city to emperor and king. . . .
>
> The forms of their sanctity are as varied as all [humankind]—men and women living lives of great austerity alone on barren islands or in deserts performing the most astonishing mortifications and penances; others living in crowded cities ministering to the needy and stricken; and still others living in castles and royal courts. Some of the saints performed the most menial tasks in almost total obscurity; others worked in the full glare of . . . prominence. . . . For the Church, like her Master, ignores the arbitrary distinctions humans make—class, race, color, position—in choosing her saints but rather selects those who in some outstanding way have devoted themselves to following the path laid out for all men and women by God-become-man, Jesus Christ.[1]

Those words are a good description of sainthood. Unfortunately, they leave an impression that the Protestant Reformation flatly rejected—that it is only those Christians who receive *special designation* and *public acclaim*

---

1. Delaney, *Dictionary of Saints*, 9–10.

who are *saints*—the ones whom artists have immortalized in paintings and sculpture, the ones who have days of the calendar named after them, like St. Patrick and St. Valentine, the ones whose names can be invoked to work miracles or guarantee safety. The words suggest that these are people to be admired for achievements and character that most of us can never really hope to match. The words imply that the saints may have *looked* like us and lived in *houses* like ours and worked at *jobs* like ours, but they were fundamentally different from people like you and me. So perhaps you and I shouldn't expect to have a faith as strong as St. Stephen, the first Christian martyr. So perhaps you and I needn't try to speak of our faith as passionately as St. Paul, the greatest missionary the church has ever known. So perhaps you and I don't have to consider giving up our possessions and living so utterly dependent upon God as St. Francis, who turned his back on his family riches and embraced the poverty in which the *peasants* of his time lived. The Protestant Reformers understood the *danger* of painting saints on canvas or chiseling them in stone or invoking them in prayer. For one thing, it might take our attention away from Jesus, our only true model for faithful living. And it might make us think that sainthood is an occupation, and one that most of us cannot fulfill. And it might give us the impression that being a saint has something to do with being dead.

It seems that not everyone who knew the apostle Paul understood at the time that they were dealing with a saint. Apparently, he and his companions were accused by some people of being holy frauds, even of being lazy. Paul had to be rough at times when church members were not behaving in Christlike ways. Paul had to speak bluntly when people were misrepresenting the gospel. Perhaps his and his companions' critics were Jews who were jealous of their following and scandalized by their teaching. In First Thessalonians, Paul felt compelled to defend himself against slanderous charges: "You are witnesses," he wrote, "and God also, how pure, upright, and blameless our conduct was toward you believers. As you know, we dealt with each one of you like a father with his children, urging and encouraging you and pleading that you lead a life worthy of God" (1 Thess 2:10–12a). Everything Paul *did* was with the hope that people lead a life worthy of God—God's character, God's purpose, God's fellowship, God's love, as we know these things in Jesus Christ. And the first place he always looked was at his *own* behavior, and his *own* attitudes, examining them to make sure that they were conforming to the Christ he so strongly sensed dwelt within him. For the *saint*, the measure of conduct and perspective isn't what *other* people *around* you are doing or saying or thinking, but the mind and words and deeds of *Christ*, who came not to *condemn*, but to *save*, not to *take*, but to *give*, not to accumulate glory for *himself*, but to point others to the glory of God.

If anyone in Jesus' time would have been considered to be on the fast track toward sainthood, it surely would have been the scribes and, even more, the Pharisees. It was the *job* of the scribes to be saintly—they were professional leaders of the Jewish faith, trained lawyers—that is, trained in the law of Moses, to teach it and to interpret it. But it was the *choice* of the *Pharisees* to be saintly—most of them were lay people without any formal training in theology who were concerned that the law expressed in the scriptures be kept in all of its strict detail. Not only did they want to preserve the law as it was written in the scrolls, but they devised a protective zone *around* the *literal* words of the law. They established a code that regulated conduct even in cases that the *law* did not specifically *address*, so that there would be no possibility of *violating* the law by *misconstruing* the law. Everything, they saw in black and white. There was no allowance for circumstances, no allowance for weighing competing provisions of the law, no allowance for compassion. The ordinances that scripture had prescribed for maintaining the purity of the *priests, everyone* was to fulfill under the judgments of the Pharisees.

But laws like not traveling on the sabbath or washing yourself in a precise way before eating worked a tremendous burden on most people, and Jesus had pretty much ignored rules about not curing on the sabbath when he had an opportunity of healing someone, and rules about not harvesting on the sabbath when he was with people who were hungry. After Jerusalem was invaded and the temple was destroyed by the Roman army in the year 70, the Pharisees were the only conspicuous religious authorities left in Israel. When the Gospel of Matthew was written, Christians were in constant conflict with the Pharisees who were trying to preserve the Jewish faith and saw in the followers of Jesus enemies to be stamped out.

It was in this tense and desperate atmosphere that Matthew reported the words of Jesus: "The scribes and the Pharisees sit on Moses' seat"—that is, they make known the law of Moses;—"therefore, do whatever they teach you and follow it; but do not do as they do, for they do not practice what they teach. They tie up heavy burdens, hard to bear, and lay them on the shoulders of others.... They do all their deeds to be seen by others.... They love to have the place of honor at banquets and the best seats in the synagogues, and to be greeted with respect in the marketplaces, and to have people call them rabbi" (Matt 23:2–7) (which means "my great one" or "my lord"). Jesus' most withering criticisms were not of adulterers or murderers or thieves—the most obvious *breakers* of the law. Jesus' most withering criticisms were of those who prided themselves in *keeping* the law.

The problem wasn't that the Pharisees did what the law required, but that they did it in order to be admired and respected and congratulated by others even as they burdened the common folk with countless regulations. *Humanly* speaking, they *looked* a lot like *saints*. But from *God's* perspective, Jesus said, they were selfishly trying to *earn* their way into heaven. They thought that obedience to God was something to be measured by their *own* standards, and the burdens of law-keeping they placed on others were for the purpose of winning for *themselves* the title "great one." "But you," Jesus said to his followers, "are not to be called rabbi, for you have one teacher" (by which Jesus meant himself), "and you are all students" (23:8) (that's what the word "disciple" means). "The *greatest* among *you* will be your *servant*. All who exalt *themselves* will be *humbled*, and all who *humble* themselves will be exalted" (23:11–12). The Pharisees and scribes undoubtedly *thought* that they were *serving* God by being God's police force. But what they were *really* doing was trying to *manipulate* God, to get a guaranteed *result* from God, to *compel* God's granting of *salvation*, by observing the law.

True saints of every age know that there is only One who is to be honored as Master. All of us in the church are sisters and brothers, equally entitled to each other's affection and respect. Many believers throughout history have lived exemplary Christian lives, and they would be surprised and perhaps embarrassed to be painted and hung on a wall or sculpted and placed on a pedestal or admired and memorialized on a calendar. *One only* deserves honor, they realized during their lifetime, and that one is Jesus Christ. As for their words and their behavior—they were only doing what *anyone* who loves Jesus Christ *should* do. And so, far from any sort of list of names that can be put between the covers of a book and stitched with human hands, we come to the Protestant Reformers' understanding of sainthood on this All Hallows' Eve, which also happens to be Reformation Sunday. A saint is anyone who is growing into the fullness of the stature of Christ—a stature which, ironically, has to do with humility, not honors, and servanthood, not spotlights. It is, in fact, the term that Paul used to express the destiny of *every* Christian—we are those who are called to be "saints," growing in humble servanthood as we focus our attention on Jesus Christ, whose *lordship* and *glory* compelled him to a life of quiet obedience and death on a shameful cross.

Today is Halloween, All Hallows' Eve, the day to prepare for giving thanks for all the saints of all the ages, most of whom never received any particular earthly recognition, their deeds unknown now to history, their names long forgotten. The saints are *indeed* "a fascinating company of men, women, and children who devoted their lives to Christ and his teachings in widely varied ways."[2] And it is to *their* ranks that *you* and *I* are *called* by *God* to be submissive and unassuming doers of God's will, diligent and modest followers of Jesus Christ—called, that is, to be *saints*.

---

2. Delaney, *Dictionary of Saints*, 9.

All Saints' Day

Revelation 7:9–17
1 John 3:1–3
Matthew 5:1–12

"Of Blessed Memory"

While standing in line to get a cheese sandwich at a luncheon following a funeral service at a church I served early in my career, one of my parishioners was standing beside me. A woman in her mid-eighties and a longtime member of the congregation, she commented to me, "Well, that was certainly a peppy hymn we sang at the end." A bit of conversation revealed that she had never before sung, and so I learned that the congregation was not acquainted with, "For All the Saints." I was astounded. I never in the least suspected that the hymn would be unfamiliar. By that time, I knew that my predecessor of twenty-five years had seldom strayed from a severely limited repertoire of hymns in the 1933 hymnal, but to realize that the members of that church—perhaps generations' worth—had been deprived of one of the greatest musical testimonies to the Christian hope left me dumbfounded and, over time, determined to permit and assist the congregation to grow in its exposure to the musical witness of the whole church.

The hymn certainly is peppy, as she said, aided by one of the most triumphant and engaging melodies ever written for Christian use. Ralph Vaughan Williams's tune *Sine Nomine* was composed specifically for the hymn text written by William Walsham How. Prior to becoming bishop of Wakefield in West Yorkshire, England, Reverend How had served a diocese that included some of the worst slums in London, on the city's east side, and came to be known as "the People's Bishop," a friend and champion of the common folk of England, well familiar with the daily hardships and struggles of his flock. But it was even before becoming a bishop that he wrote the words that speak so boldly of trust and assurance and hope about

God's assessment of all those who have been faithful to Jesus Christ in their earthly life and who now enjoy their heavenly rest, blessed for eternity in God's safekeeping, unknown, perhaps, and unheralded by those still living on earth, but esteemed as dear in the unfading memory and unfailing embrace of God. More than a "peppy hymn," "For All the Saints" gives unequivocal witness to the promise of Jesus that not one of us whose life has been enfolded into Christ will be forgotten by God, not even a hair of our head, or that we will be abandoned by God, will be condemned by God, thanks to the obedient death and powerful resurrection and everlasting love of our Lord and Savior.

Over its lifetime within the Christian repertoire, "For All the Saints" has, in fact, been sung to at least three different tunes written specifically for the text, each one stirring, each one expressing powerful confidence, but two of which fell into rather immediate disuse when Vaughan Williams set the text to his new tune in *The English Hymnal* back in 1906. In 1868, "For All the Saints" appeared in a hymnbook called the *Sarum Hymnal* to be sung to a tune called *Sarum*, which can still be found in today's hymnals but almost always paired with other texts. It, too, is bold and upbeat, but not really very memorable. The great Anglo-Irish composer Charles Villiers Stanford wrote a different tune for it, which he called *Engelberg*, when the hymn was included in the 1904 edition of *Hymns Ancient and Modern*. You may know Stanford's tune from the wonderful hymn, "We Know That Christ Is Raised," or perhaps from the magnificent "When in Our Music God Is Glorified," which was written by Fred Pratt Green as a way of preserving *Engelberg* from disappearing into oblivion, for it almost immediately fell out of favor when, only two years after Stanford wrote it, Vaughan Williams's tune virtually blew it out of the hymnic water, so to speak.

All of which is to say that "For All the Saints" has had an important place in the hearts and minds and voices of composers and congregations alike ever since it was written way back in the 1860s. Clearly, it has filled a need for Christ's church and has given strong hope and assurance to all those who have known themselves to be deeply blessed by the saints they have known, and in whose company they hope someday to be numbered, nameless perhaps to the history books but written indelibly in the mind and on the heart of God—neither wealthy in goods nor even in spirituality, perhaps, but profoundly trustful of God's goodness and righteousness; weighed down by the sorrows of the world, perhaps, but confident that Christ knows and carries their burdens and the burdens of all humankind; humble and not presuming to claim anything by right, perhaps, but welcoming and prizing each morsel and every joy as undeserved but genuine grace; craving yet satisfied with daily bread and desiring always to be worthy of God's care; looking upon and treating every human being, every living thing, as a creation beloved by and of infinite value to God and thus full worthy of our forgiveness and forbearance and sacrificial love; seeking single-mindedly to please God by obeying God's command and aligning with God's intention and thus fulfilling God's purpose by the very best use of the gift of life; willing to set aside earthly entitlements and privileges and offering one's entire self, even one's very being, to bring about the wholeness and community and mutuality for which God brought the world into existence; willing to bear the disfavor of others for the sake of being obedient and faithful to the truth of God and resisting all other claims to primacy in one's life. One alone perfectly fits that description, of course, but all who have confessed him as Lord, all who have claimed him as Savior, all who have aspired to such faithfulness as his, dying with Christ and being raised with Christ even daily, scripture calls "saints."

The book—really, a lengthy letter—that we know as the Revelation to John, or as the Apocalypse, which also means "disclosure" or "unveiling," is on the face of it a series of visionary scenes far distant from earthly reality. But, as we think more deeply about it, many of those scenes do actually reflect realities that we know from life in our own times, and the experience of the church.

> There was a great multitude that no one could count, from every nation, from all tribes and peoples and languages, standing before the throne and before the Lamb, robed in white, with palm branches in their hands. They cried out in a loud voice, saying,
> "Salvation belongs to our God who is seated on the throne, and to the Lamb!"
> And all the angels stood around the throne and around the elders and the four living creatures, and they fell on their faces before the throne and worshiped God, singing,
>
> "Amen! Blessing and glory and wisdom
> and thanksgiving and honor
> and power and might
> be to our God forever and ever! Amen." (Rev 7:9–12)

Well, we haven't seen that yet, haven't experienced that yet. Or have we—in a way, at least? "Holy, holy, holy Lord, God of power and might. Heaven and earth are full of your glory. Hosanna in the highest. Blessed is the one who comes in the name of the Lord. Hosanna in the highest!" shout those gathered around the Lord's table in every nation, people of all ages, of every language, of every color, of every condition, of every background, hundreds of thousands, hundreds of millions, joining their voices with angels and archangels and people of every time and place, centuries past, centuries yet to come, those living now on earth, those living now in heaven above, who forever sing to the glory of his name, and whose valiant daily living amid forces that would deny God's truth, deny God's wisdom, deny even God's existence, subjects them sometimes to ridicule and disrepute and perhaps even to death, but all of which has allied them to the crucified and risen Christ and has transformed their afflictions into symbols of God's loving approval, and thus they "have washed their robes and made them white in the blood of the Lamb" (7:14c), to use the language of Revelation.

> For this reason they are before the throne of God,
>   and worship him day and night within his temple,
>   and the one who is seated on the throne will shelter them.
> They will hunger no more, and thirst no more;
>   the sun will not strike them,
>   nor any scorching heat;
> for the Lamb at the center of the throne will be their shepherd,
>   and he will guide them to springs of the water of life,
>   and God will wipe away every tear from their eyes. (7:15–17)

Do we, gathered even in the shadow of the cross which is the Lamb's throne, have a shelter from the scorching abuse of the world's scoffing rejection? And do we know of a table where we are fed to satisfaction, having been renewed in the springs of the water of life, wiped dry of the tears that the day's sorrows and pains have wrung from our bodies and our spirits? In Christ, God is intimately aware of all the afflictions that are a part of the human condition. But in Christ, God bestows all the blessings that redeem men, women, children, ultimately all humankind, to God's purpose of life joyful, life abundant, life eternal in the foreverness of God's love. The world may not now count as blessings the things that God credits. But the great multitude of the saints, children of God, unrecognized as such by the world but children of God nonetheless because that is what they are by the love of God—they have known, and they have given witness in thought, word, and deed, to the truth of all that God has ordained, all that Jesus has promised, all that humankind has hoped and yearned and longed for, brought to pass through the life, death, and resurrection of the Lamb, the Son of God. Jesus knew that being faithfully obedient to God would cause his followers to be persecuted for righteousness' sake, and would be reviled and falsely accused of being in the wrong, that is, at odds with the ways of the world, its values and its claims. Such must have been the case among the faithful of Matthew's own congregation. But, Jesus assured, they in fact were, are, the ones truly blessed by God, blessed even to be citizens eternally in the kingdom of heaven, just as the prophets of old who were persecuted for being faithful to God.

And, so, back to the hymn "For All the Saints" and the tune to which we have become accustomed to singing it. "Sine nomine" is Latin for "without a name." Apparently, Ralph Vaughan Williams considered his naming the tune *Sine Nomine* as something of a joke, his commentary on the conventional but tired practice of giving names to hymn tunes, though he gave us some of the most romantic tune titles of anyone. But perhaps he was hinting at something else. Intentional or inadvertent, the name of the tune provides a modest commentary on the hymn text. We know the names of many great and heroic people of faith from the past. Some of them grace the doors and lintels of church buildings, simple shelters in jungle clearings, humble structures at lonely crossroads, modest edifices in comfortable neighborhoods, grand cathedrals in bustling city centers. There are statues, there are special days on the calendar, there are liturgies and divine exercises bearing the names of some of them. But the hymn celebrates, and today is dedicated to, the memory of those even who have no monuments, no institutions, no pilgrimages that draw the world's attention and history's witness, but who were people like our daily mentors in the faith, our daily examples of obedience, our daily models, probably unbeknownst to them, of Christ. Parents and grandparents, ministers and teachers, musicians and gardeners, friends, shopkeepers, caregivers, and all the others who make up a great multitude unnumbered by any human calculation, who now sit eternally at a great banquet table in the kingdom of God, forever feasting and giving praise to God and to the Lamb, God's own Son, in garments washed to dazzling splendor by the loving and obedient sacrifice of Christ Jesus and the grace which has worked salvation for the poor in spirit, for the mournful, for the meek, for the hungry and the thirsty, for the merciful, for the pure in heart, for the peacemakers, for those who have been persecuted and reviled just because they have sought to follow their Lord. Without names, so far as the world is concerned, they are forever distinguished from all of those who have sought to make names for themselves. Without names, but known, each one, intimately by God, who keeps each in eternal memory, honored with a seat at the heavenly dinner table to whose earthly extension we have come and have an honored place this very night, and each one a blessing to God.

Thirty-second Sunday in Ordinary Time

Spanish Springs Presbyterian Church, Sparks, Nevada

November 6, 2005

Joshua 24:1–3a, 14–25
1 Thessalonians 14:13–18
Matthew 25:1–13

"Pledge of Allegiance"

The people of Israel, the people of God, were living in a foreign land, exiled in Babylonian Mesopotamia, most of them, exiled in Egypt, some of them, faced, all of them, with the difficult task of maintaining their faith in the God of their ancestors. God had promised his people a perpetual home in Canaan. Many of them, having been conquered and carted *away* from the promised land, felt *abandoned* by God, even though their prophets explained that it was their own disobedience and idolatries that had led to the disastrous war and its aftermath. Others were fitting in to their new environment so well that they even started adopting the ways of their *captors*, including the *lifestyle* of their captors, including the *values* of their captors, including even the *religion* of their captors.

At first, it must have seemed innocuous, going occasionally to a festival held in honor of one of the many Babylonian or Egyptian gods; after all, they knew that there was nothing *to* these foreign religions. But then, as time went by, without really thinking about it, without ever intending to do so, they started regulating their own lives more and more according to the customs and calendars of the idols, spending their time and their affections and their money according to the priorities of the culture rather than according to the commandments of the God of Israel, aligning their wants and their desires and defining even their needs and relationships according to the attractions and seductions of a society based on self-assertion and self-aggrandizement. And pretty soon, the old ways, founded on the laws of God spoken through Moses, seemed increasingly quaint and naïve. And, though the people might have paid *lip service* to their ancestral faith, the God of Israel was more and more remote from their daily *thoughts*, their daily *actions*, their daily *lives*.

It was at this point that a group of historians stepped into the breach, and started writing down the old stories about a long-ago time when God had rescued their ancestors out of Egypt to free them from bondage—not just bondage to *Pharaoh*, but bondage to the things that Pharaoh *stood* for, and that had led to the oppression of an entire race in order to feed the human hunger for riches and the human thirst for power, and this same God had led the people through a wilderness of desert and mountain, miraculously and graciously providing food and water, and providing them with laws by which to live in peace and harmony and integrity, including the very *first* commandment about having no other gods before the God who had rescued them and reliably sustained them; and this same God had led them miraculously across the Jordan River, parted so that they could pass over safely, into the land that had been given to Abraham and Sarah and all their descendants many generations before, and ridded it of hostile occupants so that they could multiply and prosper and become an example for all humankind; and how their ancestors had solemnly vowed to fear and serve this God—that is, to obey God's commands, to worship God alone, to look to God's direction and provision for all their well-being. So the people of God *later* living as exiles in Mesopotamia and Egypt heard for *themselves* the words of a man named Joshua—Moses' successor—speaking to them across the centuries the words that he, Joshua, had once spoken to people who were descended from Abraham who had originally come from Mesopotamia and turned his back on *its* gods in answer to the call of the one *true* God—the people who had then just been set free from their Egyptian oppressors by the mighty miracle of this same God: "Now therefore revere the LORD, and serve him in sincerity and in faithfulness; put away the gods that your ancestors served beyond the River" (meaning the Euphrates) "and in Egypt, and serve the LORD. Now if you are *unwilling* to serve the LORD, choose this day whom you *will* serve, whether the gods your ancestors served in the region beyond the River or the gods of the Amorites in whose land you are living; but as for *me* and *my* household, *we* will serve the LORD" (Josh 24:14–15).

The gods of Egypt had proved false and ineffective; the God of Israel had bested them with the plagues, forty years earlier in the time of Moses. The gods of Mesopotamia were but idols, as they knew; they had no real substance. The gods of the Amorites, one of the tribes of Canaan, had been powerless to give the Amorites a victory; the Israelites had defeated them when they came into the promised land. Joshua's original audience knew that the choice was no real choice at all—there was only *one* God who had been true and reliable, and all *others* were not really *gods*, only creations of metal or clay or wood, fashioned by human hands from the stuff of the earth, representing only the lusts and pleasures and appetites of the world. The people answered Joshua,

> "Far be it from us that we should forsake the Lord to serve other gods; for it is the Lord our God who brought us and our ancestors up from the land of Egypt, out of the house of slavery, and who did those great signs in our sight. He protected us along all the way that we went, and among all the peoples through whom we passed; and the Lord drove out before us all the peoples, the Amorites who lived in the land. Therefore we also will serve the Lord, for he is our God." (Josh 24:16–18)

Would the later Israelites, for whom the book of Joshua was written, hear and heed what their ancestors declared and promised at Shechem so long ago? Would the later Israelites, for whom the book of Joshua was written, turn away from the idols of their captivity and shun their ways, their values and their seductions?

It wouldn't just be a matter of saying, "Yes"; of promising, "God is our God." It would require a whole way of living, a whole outlook on life and on other people and on the world around them. "Joshua said to the people, 'You cannot serve the Lord, for he is a holy God. He is a jealous God; he will not forgive your transgressions or your sins'" (24:19)—in other words, your God will brook no rebellion or disloyalty, no disobedience to his commands and no rejection of his authority. "'If you forsake the Lord and serve foreign gods, then he will turn and do you harm, and consume you, after having done you good.' And the people said to Joshua, 'No, we will serve the Lord!'" (24:20–21).

Now it was the turn of the people living as exiles from the Holy Land in Babylon and Egypt to pledge *their* allegiance to God in the midst of an idolatrous and seductive culture, a culture that rewarded *greed* and not *simplicity*, a culture that *scoffed* at mercy rather than *practicing* it, a culture that *abused* and *oppressed* the poor rather than *ministering* to the indigent and raising them *up*, a culture built on *power* and *acquisitiveness* rather than on *humility* and *generosity*, a culture that celebrated *cruelty* and *severity* and ridiculed *kindness* and *gentleness*, a culture that worshiped *things* made with *human* hands and *slandered* the Creator of the *universe*—now it was the turn of those who said they were believers in God, worshipers of God, God's own people, to turn away from the idolatrous ways of the culture around them and pledge their full allegiance to the living God who had always proved to be *worthy* of their worship. It was a moment every bit as solemn and momentous for *them*, scattered to the four corners of the earth, as it had been for their *ancestors* back in the days of Joshua when they had first entered the land of God's promise: "'You are witnesses against yourselves,'" Joshua forewarned, "'that you have chosen the Lord, to serve him.' And they said, 'We are witnesses.' He said, 'Then put away the *foreign* gods that are among you, and incline your hearts to the Lord, the God of Israel.' The people said to Joshua, 'The Lord our God we will serve, and *him* we will obey'" (24:22–24).

Just a Cecil B. DeMille moment? Hardly. We make a mistake if we think that idolatry is a thing of the past, *or* rebellion against God. It's just that idolatry and rebellion were less subtle back then—statues that were supposed to be bowed down to, yielding to the commands of emperors and kings that were direct contradictions to the commandments of God. Today, we are seldom if ever tempted by such *obvious* things. But to devote our time and our treasure and to take our marching orders from the world's -ologies and -isms, to give bumper sticker slogans and gnawing prejudices more credence than the teachings of scripture, to squeeze around the *edges* of God's commands by staking out our *own* definitions of "good" and "evil" and by somehow fooling ourselves that that *isn't* rebellion against God, well, our culture is probably even *more* adept at worshiping idols and rebelling against God than ever glittering Babylon and alluring Egypt were. Every generation of God's people, in every location, needs to acknowledge the idolatries they face *squarely*, declare what loyalty to God's commands requires of them *clearly*, and pledge their allegiance to God *unequivocally*, not just with words but with deeds, not just in general but in specifics, not just theoretically but, to put it bluntly, in the pocketbook. For that is undoubtedly the most honest indication of our allegiances, our values and our affections. And we can try to rationalize our way out of pledging our allegiance in such a fundamental way, we can try to exalt the form of our confession over the substance of our behavior, but in the end, Joshua's admonition remains true for the people of God of *every* generation and *every* location: "You are witnesses against yourselves that you have chosen the Lord, to serve him" (24:22).

The choice was still as momentous for the exiles in Babylon and Egypt as it was for their ancestors who were descendants of a wandering Mesopotamian and whom God had just liberated from Egypt. And, in the eyes of the historians who wrote down Joshua's words, the *choice* was just as *obvious*—for anybody who cared to consider the respective track records of the

God of Israel and the so-called gods who motivated and sanctioned greed and lust and oppression, could there be any doubt? And when Israel pledged allegiance to the one true God, the people of God were no longer just a group of unconnected individuals for whom God had done many good things; they became a people united in understanding and purpose who had deliberately chosen to serve this God with exclusive loyalty, no matter the risk, no matter the cost, no matter the temptations and seductions of the cultures in which they happened to reside. *God* was the sole authority upon which they would decide what was good and right, *God* was the sole comfort they would seek and cherish, *God* was the sole Lord they would love and serve.

"Choose today whom you will serve." It wasn't just Joshua's arbitrary demand. It is an eternal testimony to the urgency of not only publicly pledging our allegiance to God *above* and *instead of* every *other* claimant for our loyalty, but of conforming our life, in all of its parts, to the words of our confession. Will you serve the gods of greed and lust and oppression, which in the end are the gods of fear and selfishness and cruelty? Joshua was asking. Or will *you* serve the God who loves justice and works freedom and demands well-being for all people, the God whose *own* abundant generosity is to be honored by boundless *human* generosity, the God whose *own* undeserved mercy is to prompt infinite *human* mercy, the God whose *own* indiscriminate love empowers selfless *human* love?

The question is as urgent for us in our world, our culture, our lives in which many idols are competing for our allegiance, as it was long ages ago. The temptations and seductions are pretty much the same. But the one true God who frees and sustains and dignifies and prospers is *also* still the same. Next Sunday, we return to this place to pledge not just our *financial* support for the mission and ministry of God's Son, Jesus Christ, through Spanish Springs Presbyterian Church. Next Sunday, we return to this place to pledge our *allegiance*—to declare whom we trust, whom we will serve, to whom we belong, with our affections, with our energies, and yes, very importantly, with a significant portion—in fact, the very *first* portion—of the wealth with which God has blessed us. "Then," the book of Joshua reports, "the people answered, 'Far be it from us that we should forsake the LORD to serve other gods; for it is the LORD our God who brought us and our ancestors up from the land of Egypt, out of the house of slavery, and who did those great signs in our sight. He protected us all the way that we went. . . . *We . . .* will serve the LORD!'" (24:16–18).

Thirty-third Sunday in Ordinary Time
Spanish Springs Presbyterian Church, Sparks, Nevada
November 17, 2002

Judges 4:1–7
1 Thessalonians 5:1–11
Matthew 25:14–30

"The Memories in the Closet"

Charlotte's mother stopped as usual at the front entrance to the gardens on her way to the ferry terminal. And, as usual, she leaned over and kissed her daughter goodbye as the girl prepared to get out the passenger-side door of the old green sedan, mostly out of habit, but also out of affection. Charlotte returned the gesture with a weak smile, as usual, and pulled the large canvas bag out of the back seat, along with the collapsible wooden stool. "Have a pleasant day," her mother said as Charlotte closed the back door.

A few times, in the early days of this routine, Charlotte had responded with, "Pleasant crossings," but the new daily custom had quickly become a dutiful drudgery. Not that she didn't *like* to paint, but she would have preferred simply to lie on the couch in their apartment on the outskirts of the city, looking across the busy traffic on Blanshard Street toward the mountains in the distance. The doctor had said that it would be good for her to get out in the fresh air, but Charlotte suspected that it really wasn't about the fresh air at all—while she was buttoning her blouse that day in the doctor's office, she had been certain that she heard the doctor saying to her mother in the corridor outside the examining room something about "feeling sorry for herself." Well, she had a right to, didn't she? *She* didn't ask to be run into by that driver and be knocked off her bicycle, senseless, bruised, and with a dozen broken bones. It had been enough to knock her out of university, too, and to lose a semester's credit, and now that the summer was coming to an end, it didn't look like she would have the stamina yet to return for the fall semester, either. The stool and canvas bag were almost too much for her to handle, one way each in the early morning and again in the late afternoon.

She stood at the gate as still as a statue, waiting to be noticed by one of the gardeners, her canvas bag resting on the sidewalk and the stool leaning against the gatepost. By nature, she was not assertive, and her accident had made her even less so. "Pete," she finally said when she recognized a familiar figure passing through the courtyard beyond the gate. One rib had punctured her lung; her voice was still not strong, but, then, she had never talked very loudly. "Pete, can you let me in?" she asked, speaking up again when he had apparently failed to hear her the first time.

The middle-aged man with a flat green cap and full grey moustache turned his head, surprised to hear his name, but smiling as he recognized Charlotte. "Miss Charlotte," he said cheerily, bounding toward the gate and unlocking it. "Come right in," he added as he held the gate open and reached for her canvas bag. "The Sunken Garden today, or the roses, perhaps?"

"Thank you," she said, returning his smile, but not matching it either in breadth or sincerity. "The Sunken Garden, I think, since it doesn't look like rain." The Sunken Garden was the farthest from the visitor's center, which would have made it harder for her to retreat to shelter in the event of wet weather. On days when there was a mist or it was threatening rain, she preferred to work in the Italian Garden or the Rose Garden, nearer to the visitor's center.

"Oh, it's going to be a fine day," Pete said, slinging the canvas bag on his shoulder.

Charlotte's mother knew one of the managers of the famous tourist spot, and had arranged for her daughter to gain access before opening time so that she could drop her off each morning on her way to work as a steward on one of the big V-class ferries that plied their way from the island to the mainland and back again several times a day. The gardens were already busy long before most people were up for work, as an army of gardeners manicured the beds and lawns, and fertilized and weeded and pruned. They had become accustomed to seeing the twenty-year-old sitting on her stool in front of the portable easel applying strokes to a canvas. But they were puzzled why, whenever any of them would come near to look at her work, she would quickly remove it from the easel or throw a cloth over it. "It's not finished," she would say if they inquired about it, or, "It's not any good." People came from all over the world to paint here, but the wan face of this young woman seemed to hold none of the joy and wonder that the gardens inspired for most artists, and, at the end of the day, when she packed her paints and brushes and palette and canvas and portable easel back into her bag, there was never any indication of satisfaction or accomplishment.

There was a time when Charlotte had taken great delight in painting, had even aspired to attend art school back east. She had been painting ever since grade six, when her father surprised her one Christmas with a beginning paint set of canvas, palette, three brushes, and primary colors plus a big tube of white. That very afternoon, he had given in to her pleading, and had taken her down to the inner harbor, where she made her first effort at capturing the quay, which itself would have been filled with artists' stalls in the summertime, and the big old hotel that sat across Government Street opposite. Her parents had praised her first effort, of course, and she had gone on to paint many of the city's famous scenes until she was seventeen years old.

That was when Matthew had entered her life, or, rather, she had tried to enter *his* life. After months of hoping, Matthew had, in fact, asked her out on a date, and they had continued to date from time to time, even after the school craft fair. It was the day after she had submitted her painting of children playing in Beacon Hill Park that she saw Matthew, with two of his friends, standing in front of the picture, pointing at it and laughing. She had not picked up a brush since that day until the doctor offered his prescription about her getting out in the fresh air and her mother suggested that she take paints and a canvas to the gardens. Her father had not lived to see her set them aside, and it had taken her mother several weeks to notice that her daughter had abandoned her hobby. Charlotte had never told her about the incident with Matthew and his friends. Though they had gone to a movie together less than a month before the accident, Matthew had never since visited her or even called on the telephone. Subliminally, perhaps, that is why Charlotte did not demur when her mother made the suggestion about spending some time painting in the gardens.

Charlotte followed Pete silently along the winding path that eventually dropped into what had once been a quarry but was now a lush kaleidoscope of every sort of flower imaginable. "Where do you want to set up?" Pete asked over his shoulder. "The lupines are nice."

"All right," Charlotte responded without any hint of enthusiasm, as if she were only taking orders about how she must live life. Sensing, perhaps, that her tone might be misunderstood as rudeness, she added, "I haven't done the lupines yet."

"Sometime, I'd like to see your work," Pete said as they reached a broad grassy space between a batch of day lilies and a field of bright blue and white lupines.

"Oh," she said, "it's just something I do for myself to pass the time away. I don't think they're very good."

"Well," Pete responded, drawing the portable easel out of the bag and erecting it for her, "all of us would be interested. I'm sure your work is very good. You know, we get to see a lot of people here painting every summer. Some are probably better than others, but the point is, they enjoy it, and what they do eventually gives joy to others."

Charlotte gave no sign that she was even listening to what Pete was saying, much less heeding it, as she looked around briefly to get a sense of composition, and then turned the easel slightly and set her stool so as to get a glimpse of the water fountain playing in the pond at the far end of the garden.

"It seems to me, Miss Charlotte, that God has given you a gift." Pete's voice was gentle but full of conviction. "You mustn't waste it, and you mustn't belittle it."

Charlotte, sitting now on the stool, looked up at the gardener, squinting because of the sun breaking through the clouds behind him, then looked down again as she reached for her palette and paints. "Thank you for helping me," she said, simply. She looked back up, her hand raised to her brow in a sort of salute, but meant to keep the sun out of her eyes, her gently-curled blonde hair reflecting the sunlight back into his eyes. The look of intense sincerity in Pete's face relaxed as he nodded and turned to walk away and resume his duties.

The sunshine awakened the fragrance of the flowers around Charlotte as she sketched the scene before her on the canvas. Now and then, she saw the fluttering wings of a butterfly or heard the distant buzzing of a bee, but her attention was on the lupines and the jet of water shooting up from the pond in the background. It would be a study in blue and yellow and white, but she toyed with the idea of bringing the reddish-orange cannas out from the shadow of a willow beyond the lupines and to the right of center of her picture. Or perhaps the shadow should be retained as the sun rose higher, keeping the cannas a duskier tone so they wouldn't jar the composition. That would be the safer thing to do.

Charlotte was well into painting the clouds of a late summer's morning on the island when the first tourists happened to flow into the Sunken Garden. Apparently, a tour bus had deposited a load of retirement-age Germans at the front gate. Like their Asian counterparts, these northern Europeans were polite and well-mannered, remaining on the walkways and seldom, if ever, straying onto the lawn to seek a better vantage point for a photograph or investigate what Charlotte was doing. She was faintly conscious that whoever happened to climb the great stone promontory behind her could get a glimpse of her work, but she was unconcerned, so long as no one got close enough to pass critical judgment on her efforts.

By noon, as usual, she packed up her artists' equipment, for she was tired and the afternoon angle of the sun changed the scene too much to continue. And, as usual, she would find a quiet spot where she would eat the sandwich and fruit she had brought with her, and then read one of the books she had brought along until her mother returned from Swartz Bay to pick her up.

The following day, it was raining steadily when Charlotte's mother awoke. She knocked on Charlotte's bedroom door and conferred briefly with her daughter about the weather. As her mother finished dressing, Charlotte rolled over in her bed and went back to sleep. When she got up later in the morning, she decided to finish the detail on the lupines from memory, so that she could start with a fresh canvas whenever the weather permitted a return to the gardens. After the lupine painting dried, it would join the others stacked in the far end of Charlotte's closet. It rained all that day, sometimes hard—rather unusual for early August—and into the night, long after her mother had returned from work. The tourist-passengers had been rather surly, her mother said, the weather keeping them from going out on deck and causing them to feel deprived of a full day of their vacation.

The next day still threatened rain, but Charlotte's mother persuaded her to hazard spending the day at the gardens; if it began raining early, she could always take the district bus back to town, since the route passed by the entrance to the parking lot at the gardens. But by the time they arrived at the gardens, the sun was out. Today, the gate was standing open long before the public opening, so Charlotte was well along the path to the Sunken Garden when Pete came up behind her. "Let me take that for you, Miss Charlotte," he said, reaching for the canvas bag and relieving it from her grip.

"Thank you, Pete," she replied, her smile still faint.

"The lawn's a soggy mess by the lupines, I'm afraid," he said. "We had so much rain last night, you know."

"Well," she replied, "I finished that yesterday while I was at home. I thought of crossing over that little stone bridge to where the hollyhocks are. I'd considered doing the delphiniums before their season is over, but they don't seem to be so colorful this year."

"Oh, I'm sorry, miss, but that's all shut down today. We had a sort of calamity last night."

Charlotte turned fully toward Pete and looked at him squarely for perhaps the first time, a question on her face.

"The bridge there, over the lily pond, collapsed yesterday afternoon. We guess it was the rain, softening the ground around the foundation. There was already a crack in the mortar in the middle of it, you know, and then that bad storm last winter must have weakened it. Yesterday's rain was enough to finish it off. We're just fortunate that no one was on it when it collapsed."

"That was always such a picturesque spot," Charlotte mused, starting to walk again and looking off in the direction of the lily pond, though it was not yet visible from where they were. "That's too bad."

"It fair to broke my sister's heart when I told her about it last night," Pete said.

"Oh?" Charlotte asked, not fully attentive to what he was saying.

"She used to work here, you know—was a volunteer guide for almost twenty years after her husband died and before she got sick."

Charlotte slowed her pace, listening more closely now.

"She loved these gardens. And that was her favorite place of all. Do you know, long before she began volunteering here, she and Sam, her husband, were married on that bridge? Now, if the ground can't hold a foundation, I suppose they won't try to replace it. And, of course, even if they did, it wouldn't be the same, it was so old and charming."

"I guess it's a good thing they had wedding pictures," Charlotte said, "so that she can remember it."

"There's the pity," Pete answered. "The photographs went up in smoke before Frances and Sam ever saw them, and the negatives, too. There was a fire at the photographer's studio a few days after the wedding. Since they didn't have any pictures to look at, she and Sam came back here every year on their anniversary until he died about six years after they were married."

"Well, she at least can get a postcard of the bridge. I've seen them in the gift shop."

"Yes," Pete sighed. "I suppose so."

"I guess I'll try the delphiniums, then," said Charlotte as they descended the stairs into the Sunken Garden. "Thank you for carrying my things."

"I'm happy to do it," Pete responded. "I just wish you'd let people *see* your paintings instead of keeping them *hidden*."

From where she set up her easel and stool to paint the delphiniums, back over her shoulder to her right, Charlotte could see the rubble that was once the little stone bridge over the narrow part of the lily pond. There were workmen standing inside the yellow "caution" tape that surrounded the site, pondering, she supposed, how to remove the heavy chunks of stone and mortar without tearing up the grounds around the pond with mechanized equipment.

The delphiniums, in fact, were not in full blossom this year, and the few blooms were now fading. She rearranged her easel so that, instead, she could paint the stone monolith that protruded from the garden floor and had the little observation point perched on top that delighted both children and adults. She had painted it before, of course, from a different angle, with sons and daughters and parents and grandparents squealing with delight and oohing and aahing from its height. As she thought of the visitors' enjoyment of the now-unpopulated rock, her thoughts returned to the bridge, and to Pete's sister's wedding. Slowly, another thought came to her, one that she tried to reject from her mind, but that kept reasserting itself through the course of the morning to the point that she could not concentrate on the work in front of her. Finally, but well before noon, she packed up her equipment, deposited it with an obliging sales clerk in the public nursery, and spent the remainder of the morning and early afternoon walking around the gardens, seeing them, in a sense, for the first time—through the eyes of Pete's sister, first a new bride, and then a young widow, whose love for the spot drew her back annually on the anniversary of her wedding, and then whose loss of her beloved husband drew her back as a volunteer. About two o'clock, she came across Pete, inconspicuously raking some bark in the Rose Garden.

"Where does your sister live?" she asked the gardener.

"Near Ross Bay," Pete answered, surprised at the question. "On Fairfield Road, near St. Charles Street. 1621 Fairfield Road. Why?"

"Would you be able to meet me there this evening?"

"Yes, but—"

"Would eight o'clock be alright?"

"Yes, fine, but I still—"

"Thank you," she said, turning and running, almost, back to the visitor's center.

In fact, she was out of breath when, after retrieving her book, she sat down on a bench in the Italian Garden. She tried reading, but eventually put the book down, and strolled back to the Rose Garden. Pete was no longer where she had found him half an hour earlier. A large bush with bright pink roses on it attracted her attention. She looked at it thoughtfully, then bent over it, drawing one of the blossoms up to her nose. She smelled the sweet fragrance, and she smiled.

Charlotte's mother had not asked about the noise emitting from her daughter's bedroom, the banging and shuffling sounds that came unevenly from her daughter's closet while she made dinner for the two of them. Neither did she ask why Charlotte asked her to drive out to Fairfield Road after dinner, nor what she had in her canvas bag that she toted along. She *had* noticed a pronounced change in Charlotte's mood, a brightening in her personality that had been missing since the accident—no, perhaps even long before that.

"Here it is, 1621," Charlotte chirped with nervous excitement. The sun had not yet set as Charlotte's mother pulled the car up to the curb, and they could see a man—Charlotte recognized him as Pete—pulling weeds out of a colorful flower bed in front of the house. "That's Pete," Charlotte said to her mother as she got out of the passenger side of the car, then put her head back in, adding, "I won't be long." Her mother watched her wave to the man when he looked up, and was heartened to think that his smile must have been returning a grin on her daughter's face which had been so lacking of joy for many months.

"Frances," Pete said as they entered the front door into the presence of a woman sitting in a stuffed flowered chair, a flowered comforter covering her lap and her legs, "you have a visitor. I'd like you to meet Charlotte. . . ." He turned toward Charlotte, apologetically. "I don't know your last name."

"Ellis," Charlotte said, shifting her canvas bag to her left hand and holding her right hand out toward Pete's sister.

"How do you do?" Pete's sister answered in a voice not strong, but audible, as she shook Charlotte's hand.

"Pete told me this morning that you knew about the little stone bridge over the lily pond."

The older woman nodded, as her eyes moistened and her lower lip began to tremble.

"I'm sorry. I wish they could replace it. But I got to thinking." Charlotte reached in the canvas bag and pulled out a painting. "I thought you might like this. I did it a few weeks ago." She held it up for the woman, and Pete shifted his position to stand behind the chair, where he could see it as his sister looked at it.

"Oh, Pete," the woman said, clapping her hands together and smiling broadly now as, tears streaming down her face, she turned her head and looked up at her brother. "It's just the way I remember it."

Christ the King
Spanish Springs Presbyterian Church, Sparks, Nevada
NOVEMBER 23, 2008

Ezekiel 34:11–16, 20–24
Ephesians 1:15–23
Matthew 25:31–46

"As If the Pauper Were the Prince"

In the ancient city of London, on a certain autumn day in the second quarter of the sixteenth century, a boy was born to a poor family of the name of Canty, who did not want him. On the *same* day *another* English child was born to a *rich* family of the name of *Tudor*, who *did* want *him*. All England wanted him too. England had so longed for him, and hoped for him, and prayed to God for him, that, now that he was really come, the people went nearly mad for joy. Mere acquaintances hugged and kissed each other and cried. Everybody took a holiday, and high and low, rich and poor, feasted and danced and sang, and got very mellow; and they kept this up for days and nights together. By day, London was a sight to see, with gay banners waving from every balcony and housetop, and splendid pageants marching along. By night, it was again a sight to see, with its great bonfires at every corner, and its troops of revelers making merry around them. There was no talk in all England but of the new baby, Edward Tudor, Prince of Wales, who lay lapped in silks and satins, unconscious of all this fuss, and not knowing that great lords and ladies were tending him and watching over him—and not caring, either. But there was *no* talk about the other baby, Tom Canty, lapped in poor rags, except among the family of paupers whom he had just come to trouble with his presence.[1]

---

1. Twain, *The Prince and the Pauper*, 9 (emphasis added).

So begins Mark Twain's classic book *The Prince and the Pauper*. For well over a century, young and old have delighted in its improbable tale of the exchange of position by two look-alike boys, one born to rags and one born to rule, and the experiences that each had in the other's world, back alley and palace, and the impact those experiences had on their outlook when they again resumed the roles to which they were born. When Henry VIII died, Prince Edward became king at a young age, and history remembers him—Edward VI—as good and kind and just—a result, the legend maintains, of the days he walked the streets of London in the garb of the poor. Mark Twain took advantage of a couple of old fantasies—one, that those who rule should walk around in disguise to find out what everyday life among the common people is really like, the other, that the poor might, for one brief day or so, be treated like royalty.

In ancient times, many cultures shared myths about even the gods coming to visit earth disguised in human form to find out how they would be treated. The Roman poet Ovid put to verse the story of Philemon and Baucis, a poor couple who had grown old together. Jupiter and Mercury came dressed as travelers one day, and knocked for entrance on a thousand doors, and a thousand doors were shut to them, but when they came to the humble cottage of Philemon and Baucis, they were invited in and shown every hospitality. The modest couple sacrificed their very best for the strangers. Eventually, the gods disclosed their true identities, and offered to grant the surprised old man and his wife whatever they wished—to be keepers of their temples, they asked, and that neither would outlive the other.

The mighty and powerful walking among us in disguise—our earthly rulers, even our God; every word we say to another person a word which is actually spoken to Christ, every deed we do or fail to do actually done or not done for the King—now *that* is a notion that ought to make people charitable in both act and speech. From debates in the halls of Congress to decisions in corporate boardrooms to our attitude toward a beggar on the street corner, imagine what it would be like if we really believed that Jesus the King was in a position to say to us, "As you *did* it, or as you did *not* do it, to one of the *least* of these . . . ."

Our Gospel reading this morning is the last instruction that Jesus gave his disciples before his passion. For twenty-five chapters, Matthew has been carefully building up to these words. All of Jesus' teaching about what it means to be his follower, all of Jesus' teaching about what is required to be ready for the coming of the Son of Man, reaches its climax in separating people like the sheep and the goats *not* on the basis of whether they believed right *doctrines* or whether they went to the best *church* or whether they talked in pious *language*, but whether they fed the *hungry* and refreshed the *thirsty* and welcomed the *stranger* and clothed the *naked* and visited the *sick* and came to the *imprisoned*. Even keeping the sabbath and not committing murder and not committing adultery and not stealing or coveting, it seems, won't be as important at the judgment as whether we treated the poor and the outcast and the oppressed with generosity and hospitality and mercy.

It isn't just a general *humanitarian* sentiment, though perhaps that *also* ought to prompt us to a life of charity. It is because *Christ* is specially interested in such people—the hungry and thirsty and foreigner and naked and sick and imprisoned and the like,—just like the prophets before him testified that *God* is specially interested in such people, so much so that Jesus virtually identified himself with them. "Truly, I tell you, just as you did it to one of the least of these who are members of my family, you did it to me" (Matt 25:40). "Come, you that are blessed by my Father, inherit the kingdom prepared for you from the foundation of the world" (25:34). "Truly I tell you, just as you did *not* do it to one of the least of these, you did *not* do it to *me*" (25:45). "You that are accursed, depart from me into the eternal fire prepared for the devil and his angels" (25:41).

That is a pretty serious teaching. Are Jesus' teachings really being *taken* seriously when we hear even *Christians* say things such as "Why should *I* be paying taxes for schools for *them*?"—"them" being, oftentimes, the poor; or "Life was fine here until *they* came"—"they" being foreigners; or "If you *feed* them, you'll just encourage them to *breed*"—I've even heard *that* said by Christians; or, on another subject, "Forget all this rehabilitation nonsense; lock up the criminals and throw away the key"?—seldom said of white-collar criminals, by the way. Try as we can to spiritualize Jesus' words about the judgment, there's no getting away from the concreteness of what Jesus said here about the needy and the outcast. Hope as we might that Jesus, when he talked about "the least of these," was referring only to Christian missionaries, there is every indication that Jesus was as much concerned about the treatment of *pagans* as he was about the treatment of *believers*. And, at any rate, *Matthew* didn't build up to this crescendo as a lesson for people who wouldn't even be *reading* his Gospel; these are words of warning for the *church*—for *believers*, individually and together.

What matters the most in the conduct of the disciple is whether that person lives for *others*, and particularly others whom the world ignores or despises. And the disciple's ministry to the people the world ignores or despises should be so natural that it seems not at all extraordinary or noteworthy—it is simply our duty as we fulfill our daily calling as followers of Jesus Christ—not a matter for publicity or award, just what one *does* if one is Christ's *disciple*. Nor is individual *charity* enough. The *systems* that handicap and hobble human beings must *also* be dealt with, must be *humanized* and made to reflect the Christian values that we espouse, both in their *design* and in their *operation*. The *poor* and the *sick* and the *imprisoned* do not exist so that *Christians* will have something to *do* when they get *around* to it. Christians exist so that the *poor* and the *sick* and the *imprisoned* can be lifted from their woe, can experience dignity and wholeness and freedom, and in *this* era, that means that Christians must acknowledge the sinfulness of social and business structures that debilitate, and work to reform them—an even greater challenge when the state of the economy will be offered as an excuse to reduce charitable giving and cut services and lower wages and trim health benefits and terminate pensions for the very people who suffer most from economic downturn. No fine defense of an economic theory or political system or legal philosophy will stand the scrutiny of Jesus Christ if the result is the depredation and despair of a single person. From the products we buy to the jokes we tell, what effect does it have on "the least of these," Christ's brothers and sisters? Whatever we do to *them*, we do to Jesus *himself*.

Does it make any difference in the way we spend our time day to day to think that *Jesus* is looking *at us* through the eyes of the people we pass on the street, sit with in the lunchroom, deal with in the market? That *Jesus* is listening *to us* through the ears of people who hear us speak in our work and our leisure and our civic life? Does it make any difference in the way we spend our time day to day to think that *Jesus* is looking *for us* through the eyes of those who are sick or in prison or at the shelter? That Jesus is listening for *our* words of comfort or advocacy or welcome? And what does it mean to us that the people who will be *rewarded* in the kingdom for their kindness and generosity and hospitality weren't even *looking* for *reward*, but were simply doing as their daily duty the things that Jesus commands? Does it make every one of us yearn for a manner of kindness and a heart of generosity? Does it make us together, as a church, commit to developing a habit of mission and a zeal for service to our community and our world?

Many of us are engaged from time to time in mission—tutoring children to read, perhaps, assisting at the clothes closet or the food bank, visiting the sick and the lonely and the imprisoned. But each of us is called to make such things so much a *routine* that they are not the *extraordinary* times of our life, but a Christian *habit*.

Is what we believe important? Of course it is, and Jesus was not denying that. Is the money that we give to the church and to charitable causes important? Absolutely, and Jesus certainly was not denying that, either. But faith is only as sincere as the way we live, and even generous financial support does not relieve us of the importance of meeting our neighbor in need face to face, helping our neighbor in need side by side, loving our neighbor in need heart to heart. And as the complexion of our society changes, we may find that our neighbor *looks* different and *sounds* different and perhaps even *thinks* and *acts* different. But that *may* mean that our neighbor is even more recognizably the least of Christ's brothers and sisters. For disciples of Jesus Christ, the issue isn't race or nationality or language, but the biblical truth that whatever we *do* for a person in need or *don't* do for a person in need, we have *done* it or we *haven't* done it for Christ *himself*. And so, we really work our own judgment.

"Yes," wrote Mark Twain,

> King Edward VI lived only a few years, poor boy, but he lived them worthily. More than once, when some great dignitary, some gilded vassal of the crown, made argument against [Edward's] leniency and urged that some law which [Edward] was bent upon amending was gentle enough for its purpose and wrought no suffering or oppression which any one need mightily mind, the young king turned the mournful eloquence of his great compassionate eyes upon him and answered, "What dost *thou* know of suffering and oppression? I and my people know."[2]

"'Lord, when was it that we saw you hungry and gave you food, or thirsty and gave you something to drink? And when was it that we saw you a stranger and welcomed you, or naked and gave you clothing? And when was it that we saw you sick or in prison and visited you?' And the king will answer them, 'Truly, I tell you, just as you did it to one of the least of these who are members of my family, you did it to me'" (Matt 25:37–40).

---

2. Twain, *The Prince and the Pauper*, 207.

Evening before the National Day
of Thanksgiving

Spanish Springs Presbyterian Church, Sparks, Nevada
November 26, 2008

Deuteronomy 8:1–10
2 Corinthians 9:6–15
Matthew 6:25–33

"Keeping the Gift a Blessing"

It was a low point in the religious and social history of Judah, Israel's southern kingdom. The nation had been pulled within the orbit of the Assyrian empire, and had adopted many of the practices and had assumed the outlook of its Assyrian overlords—worshiping pagan gods, following the ways of the foreign cults, even, some scholars believe, practicing child sacrifice, as well as valuing what empires *always* value—power and wealth—and acting the way that empires *always* act—war and greed. But when the eight-year-old Josiah came to the throne in Jerusalem, the Assyrian empire was unraveling, and its stranglehold on Judah was loosening. Almost by default, Judah was now again an independent nation. And, with independence, there was an opportunity for reform. The people were ready to throw off the outward marks of Assyria's domination, including the Assyrian religion.

But the nation of Judah, while it was now free of having to bow to foreign gods and practice foreign cults, had been long alienated from its own religious heritage. And so Judah did not readily return to the ways of the God who had brought the Hebrews up out of slavery from Egypt and through the testing of the Sinai and into the land that God had promised to Abraham and his descendants. Thus it was that, during the eighteenth year of his reign, in the course of repairs being made to Solomon's temple in Jerusalem, King Josiah was given a book that had been found cast aside in some corner of the building. When he read it, Josiah was dismayed at how far the nation had departed from the terms of the covenant that God had made with his ancestors. According to 2 Kings, Josiah, cut to the heart, assembled the elders of the people and read the book to them, and they all entered into a solemn covenant before God to heed its warnings and obey its commands.

That book was Deuteronomy, and the reform that it inspired was profound. The Assyrian religion was jettisoned, along with all the other foreign religions and practices that had crept into the nation over the years, as well as such native pagan cults as had been tolerated and even promoted by Josiah's predecessors. Their priests were put to death. Fortune-telling and magic were outlawed. Rival temples and shrines were closed and destroyed. Josiah heeded Deuteronomy's urgent insistence that the nation's very life depended upon a return to the covenant relationship upon which Israel had been founded. Only by recommitting itself to God could the nation become strong again.

The book of Deuteronomy is styled as a collection of sermons preached by Moses the great liberator and prophet as the people of Israel were about to cross over into the promised land. Over and over, Deuteronomy recalls the gracious deeds that God performed for Israel's benefit. It prescribes that grateful people should respond by loving *God* and remaining loyal to him and obeying his will. It promises that, if they *obeyed* God's laws, he would bless the people with a good life in the land into which he was leading them. Otherwise, if they were *not* grateful and did *not* obey, they would be blighted with a horrible curse and would perish in the land that was intended to be a blessing.

King Josiah was thunderstruck by the discovery of the book, it seems, and devoted the rest of his reign to a thoroughgoing reform of national life. But when, in time, that nation again fell away from right worship of God and disobeyed his commands, Judah did indeed fall to Babylon, and it never recovered its former strength.

What had gone wrong? Why had Judah, the southern kingdom, with its capital in Jerusalem, gone so far astray as to be willing to embrace the ways of an empire, and a religion of idolatry? For the writer of Deuteronomy, the problem was clear: by the time the book was actually written, many centuries after Moses, the people and their leaders *had* forgotten the gracious deeds that God had done for them, *had* turned away from God and given their allegiance to other powers and principalities, *had* failed to obey God's laws, *had* become so impressed with the wealth that God had made possible for them that they began to think that it was all the result of their *own* ingenuity and labor, that it was *not* so much something *given* to them as something *earned* by them, *deserved* by them, something to which they were *entitled*, something to be *possessed*, something to be *accumulated*. What God had given them, they were no longer *thankful* for, but regarded as their *due*. The very thing that Moses had warned about so many years before had come to pass:

> Take care that you do not forget the LORD your God, by failing to keep his commandments, his ordinances, and his statutes, which I am commanding you today. When you have eaten your fill and have built fine houses and live in them, and when your herds and flocks have multiplied, and your silver and gold is multiplied, and all that you have is multiplied, then do not exalt yourself, forgetting the LORD your God, who brought you out of the land of Egypt, out of the house of slavery, who led you through the great and terrible wilderness, an arid wasteland with poisonous snakes and scorpions. He made water flow for you from flint rock, and fed you in the wilderness with manna that your ancestors did not know, to humble you and to test you, and in the end to do you good. Do not say to yourself, "My power and the might of my own hand have gotten me this wealth." But remember the LORD your God, for it is *he* who gives you power to *get* wealth, so that he may confirm his covenant that he swore to your ancestors, as he is doing today. (Deut 8:11–19)

The Bible is more than a memoir of what happened once upon a time. And the book of Deuteronomy wasn't written simply to record what Moses preached to the generation of Israelites that was finally crossing from the wilderness into Canaan. King Josiah was so overcome with a sense of penitence when he read the book that he rent his garments and set out to reform the nation's religious and social life. He saw that the people's ingratitude toward God had led them astray from what was right and good in God's sight. Ironically, over the centuries in which Israel had grown prosperous, the very *generosity* of God had come to be taken for granted. Even worse, besides forgetting the *source* of their blessings, the people had come to consider them the fruits of their own efforts and the achievements of their own design. They no longer regarded what they had *received* as God's *gift*. And so Israel no longer interpreted its *prosperity* as a *blessing*. And so Israel was no longer grateful to God. And so Israel no longer sought to *please* God. Oh, the people still gathered for the great religious festivals—kind of like people who show up in church for Christmas and Easter—but their offerings were grudging, and their concern for the poor was minimal, and they trusted in the idols of the land more than they trusted in the promises of the God who had saved them from slavery and saved them from starvation and saved them from enemies.

The importance of the Bible *today* is that it is God speaking through the *history* of God's people to provide instruction for God's people *now*. The question isn't just, What was God saying through the words of Moses to the people of *Israel* way back *then*? but, What is God saying to *us* through the book of Deuteronomy *today* about *our* wealth, about *our* prosperity? Who is responsible for the goodness of *our* land? Who is responsible for the fact that water flows and plants sprout and you and I can have life beyond the grave? And are these things we *deserve*, things that we have *bought* and *paid for*, and therefore something that are ours by *right*? Or are they *gifts*, unearned and unbargained for, and therefore *blessings*? The very dependability of God may tempt *us*, like the people of ancient *Judah*, to take them for *granted*—the fact that the sun comes up each morning, that shoots come forth each spring. And it is not such a far step from that to taking for granted even God's gift of Jesus Christ—his birth, his life, his teaching and healing, his death on the cross, his being raised from the tomb, his presence with us this very moment.

The more we have *received*, the easier it becomes to think that it has all been a result of our *own* doing. *Logically*, of course, the more we have been *given*, the more *thankful* we should *be*. The more we have *received*, the more effort we tend to invest in *keeping* it and *preserving* it. *Logically*, of course, the more we have been *given*, the more *generous* we should be. The more we have *received*, the more we have been *given*, the more *astonished* we should be that God has entrusted us with the stewardship of so *much*. And we *have* been given much, as a nation, as a church, as individuals. No one can seriously deny that. The gifts have been constant, and just what was needed. But the more we have *received*, many of us, the more *anxious* we have become, as a nation, as a church, as individuals. And, ultimately, we have forgotten where it all came from—else, why would we worry about not having enough *tomorrow*?

When our affluence, whether material or spiritual, leads us to praise our *own* skill and ingenuity rather than the creator and sustainer of the universe, when our affluence, whether material or spiritual, prompts us to be preoccupied with *securing* it rather than *sharing* it, when our affluence, whether material or spiritual, tempts us to consider it as no more than what is *due* and therefore to *despise* the brother or sister who has *less*, then we have turned the gift into a *curse* rather than a *blessing*. Then we have begun to idolize ourselves. But when our affluence, whether material or spiritual, motivates us to thank God for generosity that is *undeserved*, and to imitate God's generosity by being generous toward *others*, not just by writing an occasional check to charity but by habitual and even sacrificial self-giving, then we have allowed God's gifts to be blessings indeed—blessings through which *others* are blessed. And that was the whole point of why God chose a people for himself in the first place—so that through them, through *us*, *others* would be blessed. Thankful as we should be for God's generosity toward us, God's generosity toward us is always for the further purpose that *we* will be generous toward *others*.

It may be that people of faith will one day look back on the recent difficult economic times we have been facing as a nation, as the church, as individuals, as being itself a blessing—if it all motivates us to be more conscious of God's daily goodness and to recognize that it is all God's undeserved doing, and if it motivates us to return to living more simply so that others may also have a fair share of the earth's bounty and so that the earth itself is not abused, and if it motivates us finally to address the causes of the poverty that is so contrary to God's will for all people—if, in a nutshell, it motivates us to live more genuinely as people who are thankful. Maybe we need to rediscover Deuteronomy:

> Take care that you do not forget the Lord your God, by failing to keep his commandments, his ordinances, and his statutes, which I am commanding you today. When you have eaten your fill and have built fine houses and live in them, and when your herds and flocks have multiplied, and your silver and gold is multiplied, and all that you have is multiplied, then do not exalt yourself, forgetting the Lord your God. . . . Do not say to yourself, "My power and the might of my own hand have gotten me this wealth." But remember the Lord your God. (8:11–14a, 17–18a)

And keep the gift a blessing.

Appendix

ONE OF THE JOYS of ministry in a connectional church is to be able to share in the life of faith of other congregations and colleagues in ministry, including such events as pastoral ordinations and installations. In October 2005, I was invited by a ministry colleague to preach in his church on a milestone anniversary of ministry in that congregation. By a happy providence, the lectionary readings for that day were eminently suitable for the occasion. The event demonstrates the Spirit-inspired flexibility of the Common Lectionary (Revised). Because of the extraordinary nature of the occasion, however, I have included the sermon as an appendix rather than within the primary text of this volume.

Twenty-ninth Sunday in Ordinary Time

St. John's Presbyterian Church, Reno, Nevada

October 16, 2005

Exodus 33:12–23
1 Thessalonians 1:1–10
Matthew 22:15–22

"God in the Afterglow"

If you were reviewing resumes for the position of being the leader of God's people, or in fact the leader of any *other* nation or organization, I doubt that you would be impressed by the qualifications of *Moses*. Today, he is revered by Jews as their greatest prophet. He is certainly the most dominant human character in the Old Testament, even for *Christians*, and the *New* Testament refers or alludes to Moses and his exploits time and time again. The memory of the exodus out of Egypt, and the long journey through the wilderness, and the giving of the law on Mount Sinai, are the bedrock forming the contours of the ministry of Jesus and which outcrops here and there in explicit references to Moses, both in the Gospels and in the letters of Paul. But what personnel director or job interviewer would have foreseen such a remarkable career for a baby set adrift by his mother, who as a young man made a total mess of his first attempt at dispute resolution, who became a murderer, and then a fugitive from justice, and then, fully an adult, got a job herding his father-in-law's sheep? Someone who claimed to have heard God's voice broadcasting out of a shrub, whose public speaking skills were admittedly quite dismal, whose self-confidence and ability to be a self-starter were nonexistent, and who didn't have a clue how to go about the task that he was supposed to perform? Not really very impressive, this fellow. Surely, not even the most desperate pastor nominating committee would have returned his phone calls.

"God in the Afterglow"

And yet, it is just this same Moses whom God chose to perform the job without which there would *be* no people of God, there would *be* no Bible, there would *be* no Jewish faith *or* Christian. And that fact must give us serious pause whenever we are tempted to strike *anyone* off of God's list of potential leaders, before we disqualify *ourselves* from the list of candidates for playing a lead role in God's high-priority purpose of redeeming creation. Like Abraham the seventy-five-year-old homebody, and David the little singing shepherd-boy, and a cruel Pharisee named Saul, you and I would not have pegged Moses as God's indispensable instrument for achieving God's goal. But *God* chose Moses to be the great liberator and lawgiver for God's people, and to be God's own friend and confidant. And when we catch up with Moses in today's first reading from the lectionary, we find him debating with God, cajoling God, reminding God, calling God to account in the matter of being true to God's own intentions.

There were many occasions when Moses wondered why God had chosen him, why he had let God talk him into it, this job of leading the Israelites out from slavery in Egypt through the wilderness of Sinai and toward the promised, fabled, almost too-good-to-be-true land of milk and honey. But no incident could have been so disquieting as the faithless fashioning of the golden calf. At the very moment Moses was up on Mount Sinai receiving the Ten Commandments and all the other instructions God was giving him, the people on whose behalf Moses had been laboring were abandoning hope that he would ever return, *and* abandoning the God he had been mediating with on their behalf all that long, grumbling journey from the Red Sea. They had appealed to Moses' brother Aaron to make for them a calf out of their gold ornaments and jewelry, and they built an altar before it and made sacrifices to it and ate and drank and caroused.

God was angry, was ready to destroy them and preserve only Moses himself from whom to create the nation God had envisioned, but Moses interceded on their behalf, begged God to reconsider, reminded God that God's honor and reputation were at stake if God were to admit that the chosen people weren't worth saving. And God relented, sending only a plague and not a consuming fire, sniffing that the people could go on to the promised land but God wasn't going to have any part of it, would send along only an emissary—an angel—whereas God had originally intended to go with them personally the entire way.

Now, once again, Moses interceded on the people's behalf. An angel wasn't good enough. The people needed no less than *God* to accompany them. So "Moses said to the Lord, 'See, you have said to me, "Bring up this people"; but you have not let me know whom you will send *with* me. Yet you have said, "I know you by name, and you have also found favor in my sight."

Now if I have found favor in your sight, show me your ways, so that I may know you and find favor in your sight. Consider too that *this nation is your people*'" (Exod 33:12–13). And God seemed to give in, grudgingly, saying, "My presence will go with you"—the "you" is singular, meaning *Moses*, not *all* the people,—"and I will give you"—again, singular—"rest" (33:14). But *Moses* was proving more stubbornly faithful than *God* at this point. Way back at the burning bush, God had appointed Moses to lead the people out of Egypt to the promised land, not simply to save *himself*. And if *God* had forgotten that startling moment and the exchange that accompanied it, *Moses hadn't*. "And [Moses] said to [God], 'If your presence will *not* go, do not carry us up from here. For how shall it be known that I have found favor in your sight, I *and your people*, unless *you* go *with us*? In this way, we shall be distinct, I and your people, from every people on the face of the earth'" (33:15–16). The English here doesn't do justice to the verbal arm wrestling that Moses was engaging in with the almighty. "The LORD said to Moses, 'I will do the very thing that you have asked; for you have found favor in my sight, and I know you by name'" (33:17). Moses had won the argument.

But Moses was not yet satisfied. He pushed for one more thing. "Moses said, 'Show me your glory, I pray'" (33:18). But this was too much, or, perhaps, too little. God replied, "'I will make all my goodness pass before you, and will proclaim before you the name, "The LORD"; and I will be gracious to whom I will be gracious, and will show mercy on whom I will show mercy. But,' he said, 'you cannot see my face; for no one shall see me and live'" (33:19–20). And then comes God's famous promise to shelter Moses in the cleft of a rock while God passed by so that Moses would be protected from seeing God's face—a privilege for which Moses had not actually asked. "You shall see my *back*, but my *face* shall *not* be seen" (33:23). Not even *Moses*, whom God used to speak to face to face "as one speaks to a friend" (33:11), could look upon God's face anymore; the incident of the golden calf had tainted even God's relationship with Moses, who hadn't been *present* when the people proved so faithless. But Moses *could* witness God's *goodness*, and know the *character* of God, the *ways* of God. In God's wake as God walked down the path, in the afterglow of God's glorious exercise of divine power to bring about the divine purpose, God's having been there would be discernible. The effects of God's goodness would be recognizable. The character of God would be confirmed, and Moses could testify of it to the people.

In this episode, deep at the heart of the Jewish Torah, we have a wonderful model of a Christian pastor. Moses, who had been appointed to lead the people of God, refused to abandon them in the wilderness of their own disobedience and idolatry. In all the history recorded in the Bible, Israel never again sunk so far as to pray to a glittering statue fashioned by human anxiety. In the annals of the people's unfaithfulness, this marks the absolute lowest point. God hadn't yet had much experience with them, but God thought he'd had *enough*—was willing to incinerate the lot and be done with them! But, because Moses, whom God had searched and knew and favored, *interceded* for them, pleaded with God to *forgive* them, God decided to be *bigger* than his *anger*. And then Moses interceded for them *again*, softening God's stiff but wounded pride that would have left them alone to pick their way uncertainly across the desert toward the promised land. Moses applied psychology to God as a wise parent does with a petulant child. "Well, OK," God finally says, "but I'm doing it for *you*, not for *them*." But all the while, Moses knew, "Oh, yes, you're doing it for *them*, because *they* are *your people*." And so we learn that God takes into account the assessment of faithful individuals God knows and trusts in shaping the future, in accord with the loving and gracious divine purpose of redemption that is always God's cardinal motive. In the afterglow of the great miracle at the Red Sea, Moses knew what God's purpose was, how important it was to God. Moses knew God's goodness, God's character, and he pointed out to God that God couldn't simply destroy the very people God had saved, or abandon them—not if God was to be true to *himself*.

Today marks for this congregation and its associate pastor a milestone of faithful service, of growth, of trust, of love. I am thankful for the privilege of being asked to preach on this occasion so important to you and to my friend Scott, and I am also thankful for the providence that appointed this scripture passage as one of the lectionary readings for this particular Lord's Day. For those of us who have sensed ourselves called by God to lead God's people through the maze of wilderness that lies between the waters of baptism and the promised kingdom, and whose sense of call has been confirmed by the church, we generally have to be content with seeing God in the afterglow. In the 1960s and 1970s, it was fashionable to talk about how ministers and congregations were all equals in the task of seeking to be faithful to God, and in good Protestant terms that is certainly true in its essence. But throughout the Bible, and throughout the history of the church, some are called specifically to serve by leading, and to prepare for their leadership role specially through prayer and study and practice, and to fulfill their leadership role by more prayer, and courage and honesty and mercy and love. Throughout the story of the people of God, no one was ever *born* to lead, save one. And those who turned out to be the greatest leaders of all, including even *that* one, probably would not have been predicted by their classmates as most likely to succeed.

It's not about who we are or what we bring. It's about God's ability to *use* those raw materials, always less than perfect, and fashion us into useful, occasionally even necessary, human instruments for accomplishing the great divine purpose—the steadfast goal of redeeming the creation that sometimes frustrates God, that sometimes angers God, that sometimes baffles God, but that God always loves and refuses to abandon. And, as pastors, as leaders of God's people, it is our special task, privilege as well as obligation, to speak to God on behalf of the people, and speak to the people on behalf of God, and then to trace and point out the workings of God's faithful goodness in the afterglow of God's passage ahead of us down the road that meanders through the inevitable disappointments and discouragements and bewilderments of life to the kingdom that Christ has promised, when together we will see the glory of God in all fullness. Trusting in that very goodness, we who are called to lead the people of God learn to empathize with God's people, even when they may not be behaving very godly, to pray for God's people, even when our words seem inadequate, sometimes, on behalf of our congregations, even to dare in the midst of doubt and despair to call upon God to show evidence of the goodness that we believe is the essence of God's character. And from time to time, considering God's ways in the afterglow of having experienced over and over the great and persistent goodness of God, we may be surprised to recognize how deeply we have been known by God, how carefully we have been listened to by God, how genuinely we have been in partnership with God, how intimately God considers us to be friends.

List of Sources Cited

Achtemeier, Paul J. *The Inspiration of Scripture: Problems and Proposals.* Biblical Perspectives on Current Issues. Philadelphia: Westminster, 1980.

Ainger, Arthur Campbell. "God Is Working His Purpose Out." In *The Hymnbook*, edited by David Hugh Jones. Hymn 500. Richmond, VA: Presbyterian Church in the United States, 1955.

Bainton, Roland H. *Here I Stand: A Life of Martin Luther.* Nashville: Abingdon, 1950.

Bowie, Walter Russell. "The Book of Genesis: Exposition." In *The Interpreter's Bible*, edited by George Arthur Buttrick, 1:439–829. 12 vols. New York: Abingdon, 1952.

Brueggemann, Walter. "The Book of Exodus." In *The New Interpreter's Bible*, edited by Leander K. Keck, 1:677–981. 12 vols. Nashville: Abingdon, 1994.

Delaney, John B. *Dictionary of Saints.* Garden City, NY: Doubleday, 1980.

Dillard, Annie. *Teaching a Stone to Talk.* New York: Harper Perennial, 2008.

Fretheim, Terence E. "The Book of Genesis." In *The New Interpreter's Bible*, edited by Leander K. Keck, 1:321–674. 12 vols. Nashville: Abingdon, 1994.

King, Martin Luther, Jr. "I Have a Dream." Speech text. https://www.ihaveadreamspeech.us.

Robinson, Phil Alden, dir. *Field of Dreams.* Produced by Gordon Company. Universal Pictures, 1989.

Twain, Mark. *The Prince and the Pauper.* Signet Classics. New York: New American Library, 2002.

Wright, N. T. "The Letter to the Romans." In *The New Interpreter's Bible*, edited by Leander K. Keck, 10:395–770. 12 vols. Nashville: Abingdon, 2002.

www.ingramcontent.com/pod-product-compliance
Lightning Source LLC
Chambersburg PA
CBHW071231170426
43191CB00032B/1317